# Roger Federer

## Other books in the People in the News series:

Maya Angelou
Tyra Banks
David Beckham
Beyoncé
Sandra Bullock
Fidel Castro
Kelly Clarkson
Hillary Clinton
Miley Cyrus
Ellen Degeneres
Leonardo DiCaprio
Hilary Duff
Zac Efron
Brett Favre
50 Cent
Al Gore
Tony Hawk
Salma Hayek
Jennifer Hudson
LeBron James
Jay-Z
Derek Jeter
Steve Jobs
Dwayne Johnson
Angelina Jolie
Jonas Brothers
Kim Jong II
Hamid Karzai
Coretta Scott King
Ashton Kutcher

Lady Gaga
George Lopez
Bernie Madoff
Tobey Maguire
Eli Manning
John McCain
Barack Obama
Michelle Obama
Danica Patrick
Nancy Pelosi
Tyler Perry
Michael Phelps
Queen Latifah
Daniel Radcliffe
Condoleezza Rice
Rihanna
Alex Rodriguez
J.K. Rowling
Shakira
Tupac Shakur
Will Smith
Sonia Sotomayor
Gwen Stefani
Ben Stiller
Hilary Swank
Justin Timberlake
Usher
Denzel Washington
Serena Williams
Oprah Winfrey

# Roger Federer

## by Anne K. Brown

**LUCENT BOOKS**

*A part of Gale, Cengage Learning*

Detroit • New York • San Francisco • New Haven, Conn • Waterville, Maine • London

Brown, Anne K., 1962-
  Roger Federer / by Anne K. Brown.
     p. cm. -- (People in the news)
  Includes bibliographical references and index.
  ISBN 978-1-4205-0611-2 (hardcover)
  1.  Federer, Roger, 1981---Juvenile literature. 2.  Tennis players--Switzerland--Biography--Juvenile literature.  I. Title.
  GV994.F43B76 2012
  796.342092--dc23
  [B]
                                                                    2011026202

Lucent Books
27500 Drake Rd
Farmington Hills MI 48331


ISBN-13: 978-1-4205-0611-2
ISBN-10: 1-4205-0611-0

Printed in the United States of America
1 2 3 4 5 6 7 15 14 13 12 11

# Contents

**F**ame and celebrity are alluring. People are drawn to those who walk in fame's spotlight, whether they are known for great accomplishments or for notorious deeds. The lives of the famous pique public interest and attract attention, perhaps because their experiences seem in some ways so different from, yet in other ways so similar to, our own.

Newspapers, magazines, and television regularly capitalize on this fascination with celebrity by running profiles of famous people. For example, television programs such as _Entertainment Tonight_ devote all their programming to stories about entertainment and entertainers. Magazines such as _People_ fill their pages with stories of the private lives of famous people. Even newspapers, newsmagazines, and television news frequently delve into the lives of well-known personalities. Despite the number of articles and programs, few provide more than a superficial glimpse at their subjects.

Lucent's _People in the News_ series offers young readers a deeper look into the lives of today's newsmakers, the influences that have shaped them, and the impact they have had in their fields of endeavor and on other people's lives. The subjects of the series hail from many disciplines and walks of life. They include authors, musicians, athletes, political leaders, entertainers, entrepreneurs, and others who have made a mark on modern life and who, in many cases, will continue to do so for years to come.

These biographies are more than factual chronicles. Each book emphasizes the contributions, accomplishments, or deeds that have brought fame or notoriety to the individual and shows how that person has influenced modern life. Authors portray their subjects in a realistic, unsentimental light. For example, Bill Gates—cofounder of the software giant Microsoft—has been instrumental in making personal computers the most vital tool of the modern age. Few dispute his business savvy, his perseverance, or his technical expertise, yet critics say he is ruthless in his dealings with competitors and driven more by his desire to maintain Microsoft's dominance in the computer industry than by an interest in furthering technology.

In these books, young readers will encounter inspiring stories about real people who achieved success despite enormous obstacles. Oprah Winfrey—one of the most powerful, most watched, and wealthiest women in television history—spent the first six years of her life in the care of her grandparents while her unwed mother sought work and a better life elsewhere. Her adolescence was colored by pregnancy at age fourteen, rape, and sexual abuse.

Each author documents and supports his or her work with an array of primary and secondary source quotations taken from diaries, letters, speeches, and interviews. All quotes are footnoted to show readers exactly how and where biographers derive their information and provide guidance for further research. The quotations enliven the text by giving readers eyewitness views of the life and accomplishments of each person covered in the *People in the News* series.

In addition, each book in the series includes photographs, annotated bibliographies, timelines, and comprehensive indexes. For both the casual reader and the student researcher, the *People in the News* series offers insight into the lives of today's newsmakers—people who shape the way we live, work, and play in the modern age.

# Becoming Roger Federer

Roger Federer has everything a tennis star should: a pinpoint-accurate forehand, a powerful one-handed backhand, and a serve that has been described as technically perfect. He has been ranked as the number one player in the world, and some observers argue he is the greatest player in the history of tennis. They do so with good reason: Federer holds the record for the most wins in Grand Slam tournaments and has spent the most consecutive weeks as the number one ranked player in professional tennis.

Even beyond these record-breaking statistics, though, Federer is admired in the tennis world for his perfect form, beautiful style, and finesse. Former tennis great John Newcombe expressed his awe at Federer's graceful power:

> It's almost disturbing how Roger hits these winners [shots] then just casually walks across the other side of the court. … It's almost like you're out there with a fighter and you hit him with the best punch you've ever thrown and the guy doesn't move and then just bang, knocks you out.[1]

With such a history of accomplishments, it would be easy for Roger Federer to become demanding, spoiled, and difficult. However, he has earned a reputation as a fair player, a polite and considerate sports hero, a humanitarian, and a true gentleman both on and off the tennis court. On the court, he is mild mannered, relaxed, and easygoing. Off the court, he is kind and humble and seems almost shy at times. Yet he was not born with perfect skills and an angelic personality. Federer has worked hard at his game, his self-control, and his public image.

## An Impulsive Youth

An old saying goes, "Boys will be boys." Even Roger Federer was a boy at one time—and often behaved like a mischievous one on his journey to become a world-class athlete. Despite his current reputation as a gentleman, he admits he was not always this way. He often teased and annoyed his older sister, Diana, for example, and broke things by playing with a tennis ball in the house.

While a junior tennis player, from the age of about ten to sixteen, Roger often goofed around in practices. He also did his share of cursing, ranting, and racket throwing on the court. He struggled with impulsiveness, stubbornness, and outbursts of temper. Once, when he was sixteen years old, his impulses got the better of him while he was at a Swiss tennis training academy. He recalled:

> There was a new curtain at the tennis center. They said that if someone were to wreck the curtain, they had to clean toilettes for a week. I looked at the curtain and thought that it was so thick that there was no way anybody could wreck it. Ten minutes later, I turned around and hurled my racquet at the curtain like a helicopter. It sliced through the curtain like a knife going through butter.[2]

The tennis center fell silent as everyone stared, and the coaching staff was true to its word. Roger spent the next week getting up before dawn and helping the groundskeeper clean toilets and the tennis courts.

When Federer turned professional, he realized that his cursing and racket-smashing antics served no purpose and were

*As a youth, Roger Federer struggled with his temper and impulsive outbursts on the court. He has since developed a reputation as a mild-mannered, yet world-class, tennis player.*

embarrassing. He therefore worked for many years to control his on-court behavior. He eventually settled down and developed a reputation as a steady, controlled player. He has maintained this persona and is now known as one of the most mild-mannered, gentlemanly players in the game. As *Sports Illustrated* reporter S.L. Price put it:

> There has never been a player in tennis—much less in any sport— ... who dazzled ... [the] crowd not with tantrums or vulgarity but with quiet explosions of genius. It was never possible to be bored with Federer. ... He worked hard, adjusted his game, and came back to win ... [it] is a testament to character, a sign that real toughness always bubbled beneath the superior gifts.[3]

Since Federer became a professional, any frustration that boiled up is usually directed at himself. In postmatch press conferences, he often criticizes his own shots or technique. Rarely does he complain about bad calls or his opponent. He has acknowledged that his strongest desire is to play a perfect game, and he is hard on himself when he makes mistakes.

## A Fair Player

Many people have marveled at Federer's success, even wondering if he has found some sort of magic formula to achieve so much in tennis. Experts have studied his style and tried to copy it. Opponents have looked for weaknesses in his game in order to beat him. Yet Federer remains unequalled in style and the quality of his play. He attributes his success to hard work and a unique philosophy. Rather than focusing his efforts on eliminating or improving his weaknesses, Federer believes in building up the things that he does best. "I have always believed in my strengths," he says. "In tennis, working on your weaknesses may make you a complete player overall, but it will eliminate your dangerous edge. That's why I like to work on my strengths."[4]

Federer also understands that along with his tennis achievements, his style and behavior will be recorded forever and will make a mark on his reputation. When asked by tennis superstar Billie Jean King about the type of legacy he would like to leave, Federer mentioned nothing about trophies and statistics. Instead, he told her:

> I would like to be remembered as a fair player. I think I'm living up to that already. ... Also being polite with the people, because in life you can count on the elevator going in both directions—you always meet people twice, once on the way up and once on the way down.[5]

Roger Federer is still on his tennis journey. He still has goals to pursue, such as an Olympic singles medal, a true Grand Slam (in which a player wins the four major tennis tournaments in a single year), and achieving the most overall weeks as the top-ranked player in tennis. As he pursues these goals, he gives fans and journalists plenty to debate regarding the question: Is Roger Federer the greatest player in the history of tennis?

# Chapter 1

# Junior Tennis Phenomenon

The city of Basel lies along the northern edge of Switzerland near the borders with Germany and France. It is the third-largest city in Switzerland and is divided by the legendary Rhine River. The city has become well known ever since one of its residents became world famous. Basel owes its new recognition to its native son, record-breaking tennis star Roger Federer.

Roger's father, Robert Federer, was a native of Switzerland who worked for Ciba, a large global chemical company. While working in South Africa for a few years, Robert Federer met Lynette Durand, who also worked for Ciba. The couple married within a few years. They moved to Basel, not far from Robert's hometown of Berneck, in 1973.

Both Federers continued to work for Ciba, and eventually they started a family. In 1979 they welcomed their first child, a daughter they named Diana. Roger was born in the city of Basel twenty months later, on August 8, 1981. Although they were residents of the German-speaking region of Switzerland, Lynette was a native speaker of English, so they chose the name Roger because they felt it was easy to pronounce in English.

## An Early Start in Tennis

Robert Federer had introduced his wife to the sport of tennis while living in South Africa. A former field hockey player who was a natural athlete, Lynette took to the sport quickly, and both played regularly. After moving to Switzerland, their company sponsored a local tennis club, and the couple enjoyed playing in it. Both Federers were skilled players. Lynette participated in prestigious championships, and Robert received regional rankings. Lynette became a junior tennis coach and later worked for the local chapter of the international Association of Tennis Professionals (ATP)

The Federers wanted to share their sport with their children and took them to play tennis when they were very young. Lynette recalled that Roger was fascinated with balls from an early age. "He wanted to play ball for hours on end—even at one-and-a-half years old."[6] Young Roger quickly took an interest in tennis and showed early skill at the game. By age three and a half, he could hit tennis balls over the net. By age four, he was able to hit twenty or more balls in a row. His father described him as exceptionally coordinated for a boy that age.

As Roger grew, he developed into a nice boy who was both impulsive and ambitious. His parents noted that he sometimes

*Roger Federer was born in Basel, Switzerland.*

# Scenic Switzerland

**W**hen most people think of Switzerland, they immediately picture a scenic country wrapped within the contours of the Alps mountain range. Switzerland's position on the eastern end of the Alps gives it its signature geography: soaring, craggy mountain peaks, many of which are covered in snow throughout the year, and quiet, fertile mountain valleys that are equally hospitable to modern cities, quaint dairy farms, and every lifestyle in between. The Swiss Alps include the famous mountain known as the Matterhorn and are also responsible for Switzerland's fame as a haven for alpine sports such as downhill skiing and mountain climbing.

Switzerland is also known for its exports, such as fine chocolate, artisan cheeses (including the famous Swiss cheese), high-quality wristwatches, and the well-known multifunction Swiss Army Knife. Noteworthy citizens who were born in Switzerland or made it their home include author-architect Max Frisch; artist H.R. Giger; Johanna Spyri, author of *Heidi*; psychiatrist Carl Jung; scientist Albert Einstein; women's tennis champion Martina Hingis; and actor Maximilian Schell.

*The Matterhorn is a famous mountain in Switzerland.*

turned aggressive when he became upset, such as after losing a board game. His mother recognized that Roger often did not like to follow rules. "He was very vibrant, a bundle of energy, and was sometimes very difficult,"[7] she said. She explained that he regularly challenged his teachers, coaches, and parents, especially if he was bored or was asked to do something he did not like.

Roger's athletic nature was evident from an early age. He spent every possible moment outdoors. He tried skiing, skateboarding, swimming, and wrestling, but he abandoned these activities in favor of sports that required a ball. He played soccer, basketball, handball, ping-pong, and badminton. Sitting still in a classroom and doing schoolwork went against his nature, and Roger showed little interest in school. His grades were average at best.

## Obsessed by the Tennis Ball

Roger's parents sought ways to manage his high energy levels and calm his outbursts. They enrolled him in a local soccer club so he could release his athletic drive and learn to be a team player. They never pushed him toward a certain sport, instead allowing him to follow his interests.

Roger was eventually lured to tennis more than soccer, and his obsession for the sport was obvious. His mother recalled that he was rarely without a tennis ball and spent most of his waking hours bouncing a tennis ball or hitting it against a wall—even indoors. Their household suffered as a result, as dishes or other items were sometimes broken.

Watching tennis matches on television also became a hobby for Roger. His first tennis idol was the German player Boris Becker, who won England's legendary Wimbledon tennis tournament in 1985, 1986, and 1989. When Becker lost in 1988 and 1990, Roger, who was not even ten years old, cried over the results.

Lynette Federer considered giving her son tennis lessons herself but did not feel qualified to coach his strong talent. She knew that he needed experienced coaches who could stand up to his stubborn personality. At about the same age that Roger started school, she enrolled him in a local tennis club.

## A Complicated Personality

Roger was quickly recognized by the club's coaches as the best player in his age group. Because of this, he was allowed to attend extra lessons three times a week. Around 1987, he became good friends with Marco Chiudinelli, a boy who trained with him. The pair continually got into trouble. Chiudinelli remembered that they put more effort into goofing off than practicing tennis. "It was pretty loud when we were in training. We talked more than we trained. Training didn't seem too important to us. We just wanted to have a good time and we goofed around a lot. One of us was frequently kicked off the court."[8]

Chiudinelli described Roger as behaving very differently in practice and in competitions. He did not take trainings seriously and lost nearly all of his practice matches. In competition, though, Roger could focus and become extremely competitive. He played hard and with great intensity. The coaches and players around him were surprised that the boy who was so lazy in practices could play with such skill and focus in tournaments.

Roger's coach at the time was Adolf Kacovsky. Despite Roger's lack of commitment in practice, Kacovsky could see the natural talent in the young boy. He made the following observation about Federer's talent: "I believe Roger is ambitious because he isn't 100 percent Swiss. His father is Swiss, and the calmness Roger has comes from his father, but the ambition and willpower come from his mother [who is South African]."[9]

Kacovsky recognized Roger as a quick learner and discovered that he could learn a new skill in three or four tries, whereas other students needed several weeks. Yet Kacovsky

*Federer's first tennis idol was Boris Becker, shown here in 1986.*

# The Languages of Switzerland

One of Switzerland's unusual features is that it recognizes four official languages: German, French, Italian, and Rumantsch. These languages are spoken primarily in distinct geographic regions. French is spoken in the southwestern corner of the country by about 21 percent of Swiss residents. Italian and Rumantsch are spoken in the southeastern part of the country by only about 5 percent of the population. German is spoken by about 75 percent of Swiss residents in the northern majority of the country. As a native of northern Switzerland, Roger Federer is a native speaker of Swiss German. He also speaks English and learned to speak French while a student in Ecublens.

and others laughed to themselves when Roger, at age eight, announced that he hoped to become the best tennis player in the world. It became his driving goal, and he began to work harder at his tennis game.

Tennis began to fill all of Roger's free time. He constantly sought anyone who would play a game with him, and if he could find no one, he would hit balls against a wall for hours. He took his matches seriously and began to work harder at practices. He still struggled with staying focused and motivated in trainings, but his attitude about practices improved. Eventually, he became a ball boy for professional matches in Basel. This experience had a great influence on him. "Being there on the court with the big people, with the pros, was a huge inspiration,"[10] he recalled.

Despite his passion for the game, Roger had a lot to learn and a lot of growing up to do. From the age of about ten, he was stricken with temper outbursts. When he missed a shot or a game did not go his way, he would get angry, curse, and often throw his racket. Kacovsky and his parents helped him learn to control himself. Federer recalled:

I was constantly cursing and tossing my racquet around. I was bad. My parents were embarrassed and they told me to stop it or they wouldn't come along with me to my tournaments anymore. I had to calm down but that was an extremely long process. I believe that I was looking for perfection too early.[11]

## A Future Star Begins to Rise

When he was eight, Roger entered his first major tournament with his regional tennis club. Although he lost then, over the next three years his tennis game began to come together. He started

# Marco Chiudinelli

**B**orn in Basel, Switzerland, thirty-three days after Roger Federer, Chiudinelli was Federer's first tennis friend. The two met at a tennis club in Basel when they were about six years old. They spent so much time horsing around that they were regularly sent to the sidelines during practices.

Despite their poor training habits, both went on to tennis fame. Chiudinelli turned professional in 2000 and had a respectable career in professional tennis. From the end of 2006 until August 2007, the ATP ranked him anywhere from 135 to 191. In September 2007, however, his rank slipped to 287 and continued to drop until it reached a low of 737. Chiudinelli underwent knee surgery in November 2007, and he did not play for most of 2008 while he recovered. He reentered tennis ranked number 884 and steadily improved until October 2009, when he was ranked 100. He stayed in the top 100 until November 2010, and during this time he achieved his career-best ranking of 54.

In 2009 Chiudinelli received the Comeback Player of the Year Award from the ATP. The trophy was presented to him by his lifelong friend, Roger Federer.

winning more matches than he lost. At age eleven, in 1993, he won the Swiss national title in the indoor division for players age twelve and under. At the similar outdoor competition six months later, he again won the title. Those tournaments were crucial moments in Roger's progression as a player. He remembered feeling that he truly had a chance to succeed in the sport and that he had the ability to compete.

In 1993 Roger was introduced to another coach, Peter Carter, at his tennis club. Carter could see the boy's natural talent from the first time he watched Roger play. "His talent was instantly visible," Carter recalled. "Roger could do a lot with the ball and the racquet at a very young age."[12] He observed that Roger had an excellent feel for the ball, a good forehand, and was a fast learner. Carter discovered that Roger spent time watching tennis players on television, especially Boris Becker and Pete Sampras, and

*By the age of eleven, Federer was avidly watching tennis pros, such as Pete Sampras, on television so he could study and imitate their techniques.*

could study and imitate some of their techniques. Roger and Peter Carter turned out to be an excellent match. Roger progressed so much that his ranking rose enough to make him eligible to play in international junior competitions.

Over the winter of 1994–1995, Roger's parents and Carter considered allowing him to attend the Swiss National Tennis Center for more thorough coaching and training. Students at this academy lived with host families and attended public school part time. Meanwhile, they received intensive instruction in tennis techniques and were offered opportunities to compete.

Roger visited the academy to take the entrance examination, and he qualified for admission. This was the beginning of an exciting but stressful time for him. The Swiss National Tennis Center was located in Ecublens, in the far southwest corner of Switzerland, about 115 miles (185km) from Basel. The distance from home was not as significant for Roger as the difference in culture. Ecublens was located in the French-speaking region of Switzerland, and he spoke only German and English.

# Elite Training for the Budding Phenomenon

In the fall of 1995, just after turning fourteen, Roger moved to Ecublens. The three-hour train ride delivered him to a completely different world. He moved in with a host family and faced many new challenges. He later described the first five months of his time in Ecublens as completely miserable. "It was very difficult in the beginning as I didn't speak the language, was very homesick and had only few friends."[13] As a result, he had trouble focusing and staying motivated.

Roger was placed with a host family who did their best to make him comfortable. The Christinet family found him easy to get along with, and they understood the difficulty of his situation. Cornelia Christinet, his host mother, spoke German and helped him communicate. The family allowed Roger to call home often to talk to his parents. On Fridays he would ride the train home for the weekend to spend time with his family and friends.

The tennis academy proved to be a challenge. Roger was one of the youngest and smallest players, and he struggled to keep up with older, stronger opponents. Yet his parents and host family noticed that he never considered quitting. He seemed determined to stick to his goal of becoming the best tennis player in the world.

As the months went by, Roger began to settle in. He became good friends with his host brother, Vincent. He lost a number of tennis matches but eventually started winning. In 1996 he won the Swiss national title in the sixteen-and-under division. This was followed by a number of victories that led up to wins in both the indoor and outdoor 1997 Swiss national junior championships in the eighteen-and-under division. Roger was rising to the top of the Swiss junior tennis world.

## Another Step Toward the Pros

Roger's time at Ecublens ended in 1997 when the new Swiss National Tennis Center opened in Biel, about halfway between Basel and Ecublens. Roger was not only invited to train at the new, modern facility, but his former coach, Peter Carter, was hired to work there. An insider admitted that he had been hired purely for Roger's benefit, since so many of the staffers could see the incredible potential in him. They hoped Carter's presence would nurture his game. Roger also worked with a coach named Peter Lundgren while at the new facility.

Although Roger was only sixteen, his parents made arrangements for him to live in an apartment with nineteen-year-old Yves Allegro, a fellow tennis student. The boys got along well and took their training seriously, and their lifestyle was not wild or unruly. Their free time consisted of video games, television, and watching soccer matches from the balcony of their apartment, which overlooked a soccer field.

Roger's talent continued to develop under Carter's guidance. In early 1998 he won the Victorian Junior Championships in Australia and placed well in other international junior tournaments. His biggest moment came when he played in the

*In 1998, Federer played the grass courts of Wimbledon, winning the Junior Championship.*

Wimbledon Junior Championships in July 1998. Playing at Wimbledon had been a dream for Roger since he was very young, because it is one of the most famous and prestigious competitions in the history of tennis. Roger played with maturity and intensity, and he won all of his matches to take the title as Wimbledon junior champion. His week on the English grass courts got even better when he won the junior doubles championships with partner Olivier Rochus.

## Thrust into the Spotlight

As the Wimbledon junior champion, Roger was offered a place in the Swiss Open tournament in Gstaad, Switzerland, in the week following Wimbledon. This time-honored tournament is very prestigious, and it offered him his first chance to play in a professional tournament.

The Swiss Open was a great challenge for Roger. He was among the youngest players in the tournament, and he played against world-class athletes rather than inexperienced junior players. The clay tennis courts were characteristically slippery. Even the altitude was a factor; at 3,000 feet (914m) above sea level, the thin air meant that balls bounced higher and players tired more easily.

Roger was a magnet for the media. A press conference was held so reporters could learn more about the new junior Wimbledon champion. The grandstands for his tennis match were filled beyond capacity. The tennis world awaited the chance to evaluate the junior player in his first appearance in a professional ATP match.

Roger was defeated in his first match by Lucas Arnold of Argentina, but the experience taught him a lot. "I competed very hard, but did not play well," he said. "You have to do more running with the professionals than with the juniors and pros are not going to make as many mistakes."[14]

The tournament gave Roger a great deal of attention, but none of it was perhaps so important as the notice of Stéphane Oberer, captain of the Swiss Davis Cup tennis team. Oberer sought a way to mentor Roger, feeling that he would reach his full potential in about five years. He invited him to work with the Davis Cup team as a practice partner. This gave Roger valuable experience playing against professionals. He also continued to train and travel with his coach, Peter Carter, and the two were together constantly because of the demanding schedule.

## Moving up the Ranks

Roger's dream for 1998 was to finish as the number one ranked junior player. He was ranked as the number three junior following his win at Wimbledon and was number 878 in overall ATP rankings. That September in Toulouse, France, he entered his second ATP tournament. He not only qualified for the tourna-

*Federer's next challenge was to play on the slick clay courts of the Swiss Open in Gstaad, Switzerland.*

ment but defeated two professional players to advance to the quarterfinal round. Although he lost that match, his performance paid off; after the tournament, his ATP ranking jumped to 396. His junior ranking, however, remained at number three.

Roger played at several other tournaments with mixed results, but his sights were set on the junior international Orange Bowl tournament in Florida in December 1998. This event was his chance to advance his junior ranking. He narrowly won his first round, then created some trouble for himself. While training the next day he clowned around by jumping rope like a monkey. He took a wrong step and badly sprained his ankle.

With his foot swollen and bandaged, Roger turned into the serious, competitive player that Marco Chiudinelli had recognized years earlier. He focused his energy and managed to win his next three matches, which moved him to the semifinals. With his ankle nearly healed, he defeated two more opponents to win the championship—and he celebrated by visiting a salon and having his hair dyed blond in order to satisfy a bet. He said, "When I went to the Orange Bowl, a friend said that if I won it, I had to dye my hair. At first,

# The Association of Tennis Professionals

In 1972 a group of tennis players got together with the idea of forming a players' association for the betterment of the game. Soon, the Association of Tennis Professionals (ATP) was born. Since its beginning, the ATP has relied heavily on input from players. It gives them a voice in the management of their own sport through a Player Council. From 2008 to 2011 Roger Federer served as president of this council.

The ATP maintains a computerized ranking system that provides a fair analysis of each player's performance and assigns an objective rank to each player. This helps ensure fair placement in tournaments. The ranking system was established in August 1973 and is the official system for ranking players in men's tennis.

In 1988 the ATP put forth a proposal to design a new circuit of tennis matches. This proposal was overwhelmingly supported by players, and the ATP Tour was established. A new tour calendar was set up allowing for an eight-week off-season. The tour includes seventy-six tournaments in twenty-eight countries. In addition, the ATP maintains a player pension fund, and in 1985 it established a drug-testing rule for players.

I thought, it's too bad I won, but I've gotten to like it."[15]

Days later, when junior rankings were updated, Roger was jubilant to see his name move into the number one ranking. He finished 1998 as the top junior tennis player in the world at age seventeen. He had nothing left to accomplish as a junior player, and he knew that 1999 would be the year to make his move into professional tennis.

# Chapter 2

# Federer Steps Up to the Pros

Roger Federer had been setting goals for himself since he was eight years old, and he had accomplished several of these by the end of 1998. He was not only a Swiss national junior champion, but he was the number one junior tennis player in the world. By reaching the peak of junior tennis, he knew he was ready for the next step: entering the world of professional tennis.

At the dawn of Federer's professional career, in January 1999, his ATP ranking was 301. His goal was to finish the year with a ranking above 200 and to learn how to win at the professional level. He would not only achieve that goal but far surpass it.

## An Uphill Battle

As a seventeen-year-old tennis player in his first year competing against professionals, Federer faced enormous odds. He was young, not very muscular, and inexperienced with the intensity and speed of professional competition. Yet he refused to be intimidated, and he faced his new challenges head on.

In his first event as a professional in Heilbronn, Germany, Federer played well enough to raise his rank to 243. He won a total of six matches to reach the semifinal round, defeating a number of older, more experienced, and higher-ranked players. Federer's professional career was off to an excellent start.

*In his first round of play in the Open 13 tournament, Federer beat reigning French Open champion, and ATP 5th ranked, Carlos Moyá, shown here. He went on to lose in the quarterfinals.*

A major moment of 1999 came in February at the Open 13 tournament in Marseille, France. In his first round of play, he faced the reigning French Open champion, Carlos Moyá of Spain, who was ranked number five. In an astonishing upset, Federer won the match. He continued winning and reached the quarterfinals, but he lost that match. Still, his defeat of Moyá was a sign that Federer had a future in tennis. He recalled that important win: "It was an amazing feeling. I always felt on a big court I could do some damage, maybe not in the entire tournament but at least in one given match."[16]

# Tennis Scoring

**T**ennis has a scoring system like no other game. A tennis match is determined by the winner of two sets out of three (except in the men's Majors tournaments, where it is three sets out of five). Each set is won by whoever gets to six games first (and wins by two games). A score of zero is called "love," and a game is played to four points. Rather than counting points as 1, 2, 3, and 4, however, they are designated 15, 30, 40, and game, and games must be won by two points.

A tie occurs at 40, when the score is called "deuce" (40-40). The next player to score is said to have "advantage." The server's score is always stated first, so the score if the server was winning would be "ad–in"; if the opponent was winning, it would be "ad-out". If the person in the lead scores the next point, he or she wins the game. If the opponent scores, the score returns to deuce. Games can alternate from deuce to advantage–40 many times if players continue to tie and then pull ahead by only one point.

*A tennis match is determined by scoring games and sets.*

At a tournament in Rotterdam, Netherlands, that same month, Federer also reached the quarterfinals. By the end of the month, his success launched him ahead in the ranks; he leaped to number 129. In only the second month of his professional career, he had surpassed his goal for the entire year.

## An Uneven Start

Just as a tennis ball has its ups and downs, Federer's success in his first year as a professional was also tempered by disappointments. His indoor tournaments were showing great results, but his outdoor events were going poorly. At all seven outdoor tournaments in which he competed that year, he lost in the first round of play. Another of his challenges in 1999 was mastering competitions on clay courts, which gave him more trouble than grass or hard courts.

Federer went on to play the Davis Cup in Switzerland that April, an exciting opportunity since the event was in his home country. In May and June he played the French Open, one of the biggest tournaments of the entire tennis year. He amazed the crowd with his style and skill, especially an impressive, nearly backward blind smash that won him a point and left his opponent, Patrick Rafter, shaking his head.

July took Federer back to England to play at Wimbledon for the second time. The tennis world paid attention as the reigning junior Wimbledon champion stepped onto the court, but was disappointed when he was defeated in his first match. Tennis great Pete Sampras defeated all opponents to win the trophy and claim his sixth Wimbledon victory. Despite the loss, Federer finished the year on an upswing. In a tournament in late October 1999 in Brest, France, he seized his first professional title by winning the final match.

Federer played in a total of twenty-three tournaments in 1999. He made steady progress up the ATP rankings and finished the year with an unexpected ranking of sixty-five, far exceeding his goal to rank above 200. He was also the youngest player in the top 100 of the ATP rankings for 1999.

# Continuing His Climb in 2000

Federer was still adapting to the world of professional tennis. In 2000 he faced a hectic schedule, playing in twenty-nine tournaments plus the Olympic Games in Sydney, Australia. As a rising tennis star, he attracted media attention and frequently had to give interviews or attend press conferences. Keeping up with his tournament schedule, improving his tennis game, and learning how to respond to the media resulted in an overwhelmingly busy year for the eighteen-year-old.

Federer also had to adjust emotionally and mentally to his new role as a tennis professional. As a junior player, he had won most of his matches. As a professional, though, he lost more matches than he won. This sometimes affected his confidence, but Peter Carter continued to encourage him and made sure that Federer learned from his defeats.

Another change for Federer was a new level of control in his games. After the angry outbursts that had plagued his early tennis years, he had worked with his coaches, parents, and a sports psychologist to avoid exploding on the court. As he matured, he

*In 2000, Federer played in twenty-nine tournaments, plus the Olympic Games in Sydney, Australia.*

# The Longest Tennis Game in History

In tennis a player must win a set by two games, so a score such as 6–5 is not possible. Opponents play until one competitor pulls ahead by two games, with scores such as 6–4, 11–9, or 16–14. Because of this, set scores can go quite high. The record for the longest set of tennis occurred in 2010 at Wimbledon between Nicolas Mahut of France and John Isner of the United States. The set stretched over three days and was finally won by Isner with a final score of 70–68, for a total of 138 games.

calmed down and gained control of his behavior. Federer felt the change in himself once he reached the pros. "As time went by, I started to relax," he said. "You get on center courts around the world, people are watching, and you're like, 'Well, now I can't throw my racquet,' because it's embarrassing. Today I'm much more in control of myself."[17]

After Federer finished 1999 ranked number sixty-five by the ATP, his goal for 2000 was to finish in the top fifty. Once again, he surpassed his goal. Although Federer won no tournament titles in 2000, he had a solid year that moved him up the rankings ladder. He managed two second-place finishes, won thirty-six of his sixty-six matches, and finished the year ranked at number 29. The highlight of his year was meeting his new girlfriend, Miroslava Vavrinec, better known as Mirka, during the Olympics. The pair kept their relationship a secret for several months before it was discovered by reporters.

## An Unexpected Change in Direction

Of all the activity that Federer experienced in 2000, one decision weighed more heavily on him than any other. The big surprise that he announced that year was his decision to change coaches.

Federer had learned a great deal from Peter Carter, and they were very fond of each other. His game had improved, and his career was on the rise. To tennis observers, the situation between the two men seemed perfect. Yet after long and difficult deliberation, he chose to work instead with Peter Lundgren, with whom he had trained at the tennis center in Biel. Federer explained that he considered the men to be nearly equals, but something told him to work with Lundgren. He had the greatest respect and appreciation for Carter and said, "I think he has had the most influence on my game as a coach. ... And he really actually, I think, [taught] me the beautiful technique I play today."[18]

Observers noted that Carter seemed disappointed but accepted the situation gracefully and continued to coach for the Swiss Tennis Federation. Members of the media were stunned. Changing coaches was a surprising decision, especially since Federer was making steady progress up the ATP ranks and the two men were close friends.

## Chasing the Dream of the Number One Ranking

In 2001 Federer continued to prove he was a talent to watch. That year, he won forty-nine of seventy matches and ended the year ranked number thirteen. He also won a single first-place ATP title at the Milan Indoors tournament in 2001.

Federer's most notable moment in 2001 came at Wimbledon. The tournament was his fourth appearance on the legendary London courts. He made headlines by beating Pete Sampras, the reigning Wimbledon champion who was ranked number five, in the fourth round. It was a major upset that would be talked about for many years.

Even Federer was surprised; Sampras was one of his idols. Following the match, Federer said: "It was weird, you know, I look on the other side of the net ... I was like, it's just true ... that this is happening now, that I'm playing against him. ... Obviously something special for me to play Pete."[19] Though Federer did not win Wimbledon (the trophy went home with Croatian

*A dejected Pete Sampras hangs his head after losing his fourth-round match against Roger Federer at Wimbledon, in 2001.*

Goran Ivanišević), beating Sampras was a major achievement for him.

As many of his friends and coaches had predicted, Federer was quickly advancing to the top of the tennis world. Tennis great Andre Agassi commented: "He's young and explosive and has a powerful game. He has some of the best hand speed on the tour and he knows how to put pressure on you. There are a lot of things he does well."[20] In 2002 Federer continued to perform. That year he won fifty-nine of eighty-one matches and was ranked number six. He also grabbed three titles at the Adidas International tournament in Australia, the Masters Series Hamburg in Germany, and the CA Tennis Trophy in Austria.

## A Sudden Tragedy

Federer's life had many high points, but August 1, 2002, delivered unimaginable tragedy to the twenty-year-old. While in Canada for the Tennis Masters tournament, he learned that his former coach and good friend, Peter Carter, had been killed while driving through a nature park in South Africa. His vehicle had swerved to avoid an oncoming minibus, broke through a bridge railing, and plunged into a shallow ravine, landing on its roof. Carter and the driver were killed instantly. Federer was overwrought, and for several hours he wandered the late-night streets of Toronto in disbelief.

Federer was scheduled to play doubles in the Masters tournament the next day. He played despite his grief, wearing a black armband and clearly upset. He and his partner, Wayne Ferreira, lost their match. Federer traveled directly to the Masters Series in Cincinnati for his next tournament, but he could not concentrate and lost his first round. He then went home to Switzerland to prepare for Carter's funeral.

Six days after his twenty-first birthday, Federer attended the funeral of his beloved friend. He said that the event changed his perspective about life. At times he felt that tennis was meaningless compared to the loss of someone he admired so much. At other times he wanted to work harder and make his career meaningful to honor his former coach. In an interview on the second anniversary of Carter's death, Federer revealed that the loss was still extremely painful.

"Certainly Peter is still very strong in my heart and in my memories," he said. "And I still can't get over what happened. ... I still think of him every day. And whenever I win, particularly big matches ... I'm thinking of him for sure."[21]

## Getting His Game Back

Federer struggled with his grief at his next few tournaments. He attended the TD Waterhouse Cup in New York but was eliminated in the first round. His next stop was the U.S. Open in New York, where he won three matches but was eliminated in his fourth match, even though he played extremely well. Finally, at the Davis Cup in Morocco, a team event, Federer won his two matches, and his team was jubilant.

Federer was beginning to get his game back. His ranking, which had gone as high as number eight in May 2002, slipped

*After losing his rank for much of the season, Federer came back to win the CA Tennis Trophy, which he dedicated to former coach and friend Peter Carter.*

to number thirteen in August and September, following Carter's death. In October his focus seemed to return, and his ranking again rose to number eight. Federer's confidence was gradually returning as well. In Vienna, Austria, in October, after winning the CA Tennis Trophy, he dedicated his title to Peter Carter. After this win, his ranking rose to number seven.

Despite the tragedy, Federer managed to achieve his goals for 2002. He won a coveted place in the Tennis Masters Cup in Shanghai, China, reserved for the top eight players in the sport. After the tournament, the final of the year, his ranking stood at number six. His dream of reaching the number one ranking in tennis was closer than ever, and his grief over Peter Carter was just beginning to subside.

## The Goal of a Grand Slam

The year 2003 began more optimistically for Federer. Ranked number six in the world, he had proved himself as a true competitor. His goal for the year was to win one of the four Grand Slam tournaments held each year—the Australian Open, the French Open, Wimbledon, and the U.S. Open. These have long been considered the most prestigious tournaments in tennis, and they bear the most weight on ATP rankings. In fact, tennis players are rated not just on their ATP ranks, but on the number of wins they collect in Grand Slam events. As of 2003 Federer had become known as the best player in tennis who had not yet won a Grand Slam event. He felt the time had come to change that.

His first chance for a Grand Slam win came in January 2003 at the Australian Open. He advanced to the top sixteen round, but then lost. The first of the year's opportunities for a Grand Slam win had slipped through his fingers. The second opportunity similarly evaporated at the French Open in May, when he lost his first match. The tennis community puzzled over his performance. Pete Sampras was one of many who felt that Federer had all the potential to win a major tournament. "Roger doesn't have any holes in his game and he's a great athlete," he noted. "He's got all the tools."[22] On the other hand, René Stauffer, a tennis correspondent for a Zurich, Switzerland, newspaper, expressed his doubts about Federer's abilities: "He doesn't have [Australian tennis champion Lleyton] Hewitt's fighting spirit. We haven't seen him put his heart down there on the court."[23]

# The Grand Slam

The Grand Slam describes four major tennis tournaments: the Australian Open, the French Open (often called Roland Garros, for the name of the stadium in which it takes place), Wimbledon, and the U.S. Open. These tournaments are the most important of the tennis year, as they carry the most weight in ATP rankings. They also command the most prestige and offer the greatest prize money.

A true Grand Slam occurs when a player wins all four events in a single year. Only two men in the history of the Grand Slam have accomplished this feat: Don Budge in 1938 and Rod Laver in 1962 and 1969. Three women have won the Grand Slam: Maureen Connolly Brinker in 1953, Margaret Court in 1970, and Steffi Graf in 1988. Graf enhanced her Grand Slam by winning an Olympic Gold medal in the same year, giving her the distinction of being the only player ever to win a Golden Grand Slam.

The term *Grand Slam* has also come to refer to the four tournaments themselves; a player who wins at Wimbledon, for example, is said to have won a Grand Slam tournament. Players are also recognized for winning all four tournaments over their careers and are said to have achieved a Career Grand Slam.

June 22 brought Wimbledon, Federer's third opportunity for a Grand Slam win. He advanced easily through the first four rounds, making a win seem possible. In the quarterfinal he achieved a quick victory and moved ahead to the semifinal. Pitted against Andy Roddick of the United States, the first set was long and hard fought, but Federer prevailed. He won the next two sets, giving him the match, and he moved into the championship game of the final round. A Wimbledon win was within his reach for the first time.

## "An Absolute Dream for Me"

Reporters described Federer in the final match as playing with strength, speed, and ease. Tennis great Boris Becker praised Federer's all-around technique, saying, "He can serve and volley, can stay back, can slice and play the drop shot. He is a good example [that] you don't need a 135mph serve or heavy top spin to become a top player."[24] Throughout the championship match, Federer appeared remarkably calm and in control. His focus paid off: He beat Philippoussis and won Wimbledon, earning his first Grand Slam victory.

After the final point, Federer's emotions finally spilled forth. He walked to his courtside chair and began to weep. He described his emotions as not just joy, but relief. "There was pressure from all sides—also from myself," he said. "It's an absolute dream for me. I was always joking around when I was a boy: 'I'm going to win this.'"[25] But win he had, and it provoked a powerful emo-

*Federer kissing his trophy after winning the finals match against Australian Mark Philippoussis in the 2003 Wimbledon Championships.*

tional response. Mixed in, too, were thoughts of Peter Carter.

Federer lost his fourth opportunity for a Grand Slam title in 2003, when he did not win at that year's U.S. Open. But with a Wimbledon win, he had experienced the best year of his professional career to date. He played in twenty-six tournaments in 2003—slightly more than two per month. He won seventy-eight of his ninety-five matches, a significant improvement over 2002. Thanks to a number of wins, including the selective Tennis Masters Cup in November, he finished 2003 as the number two player in the world. His lifelong dream of becoming the number one player in tennis remained only a single ranking away.

## More Dreams Come True

As 2004 got underway, Federer was hitting his peak. After struggling for a Grand Slam win for much of 2003, he began 2004 by winning the Australian Open. He reacted to his second Grand Slam win by saying, "It's just unbelievable. You know, you come here, you prepare, you leave after three weeks basically, and you're finally the winner after such a long time. It just really feels good."[26]

That victory at the Australian Open accomplished another of Federer's goals. On February 2 he moved into the number one ATP position. The dream he had pursued since he was eight years old had finally been achieved. He said: "I wanted to enjoy this moment. You only get to be No. 1 once." With his typical modesty, he also remarked, "Becoming No. 1 was a goal but winning the title was bigger."[27]

After winning the Australian Open, he set his sights on conquering more Grand Slam tournaments. By the end of the year, he had the tennis world buzzing about his success. Following his win at the Australian Open, he took home the trophy at Wimbledon for the second year in a row. He also made headlines when he won the U.S. Open for the very first time. Suddenly, the number one player in tennis was the owner of four Grand Slam titles and had won three of the four Grand Slam tournaments at least once. The only one that eluded him was the French Open.

Although he lost this tournament in 2004, observers speculated that the final Grand Slam win was surely in the player's future.

As attention turned to 2005, sports reporters and tennis fans hotly debated the question: Could Roger Federer win all four Grand Slam tournaments in a single year to pull off a true Grand Slam? The feat had not been accomplished since Australian player Rod Laver won all four tournaments in 1969. Lleyton Hewitt, who was ranked number three at the end of 2004, was among many who believed Federer was the player for the job. "There's no doubt Roger's got the game to do it,"[28] he said. American tennis analyst and former top-fifty player Patrick McEnroe agreed: "He's got the best shot at it [because] he's the most well-rounded player I've ever seen."[29]

As 2004 drew to a close, Federer had much to be happy about. He had won seventy-four of his eighty matches, meaning he won 92.5 percent of his contests. He took home titles from eleven of the nineteen matches he played in, including the Masters Series Hamburg, Tennis Masters Series Canada, and Tennis Masters Cup. He had a firm grip on his number one tennis ranking. He also had four Grand Slam trophies to admire, as well as many others. Like many tennis fans and observers, he also began to ask himself the question: Could a true Grand Slam be in his future?

# Chapter 3

# The Pursuit of Gold

The world of sports is filled with many prizes, trophies, and awards. Yet no prize is so widely coveted across many sports as an Olympic medal. Even athletes such as Roger Federer, who are at the top of their game and hold many major titles, look at the Olympics as the ultimate prize. Federer has made three trips to the Olympics in his career, and those journeys offered many exciting twists and turns.

## The Hunger for the Olympics

The Olympics live in the dreams of many athletes. Competing and winning in the Games is special for several reasons. Because they are held only every four years, timing is important—athletes must be physically and mentally ready to compete when the Olympics come along. An athlete who has a bad year is not able to try again the following year but must wait a full four years and hope to still be in peak condition.

Another special aspect of the Olympics is the great number of athletes who participate from all around the globe. At the 2008 Games in Beijing, China, for example, nearly eleven thousand athletes from 204 countries participated in 302 events. No other event in the world draws together such a diverse group of athletes in a single place.

The Olympics are also unique because they are regarded as a

*The Olympics are unique as athletes come from around the globe to compete in more than three hundred events.*

symbol of world peace. The athletes who come together participate with a sense of fairness and healthy competition regardless of their opponents' nationality. Many countries represented at the Olympics have fought wars against each other in the past—some even have ongoing tensions with each other. Yet the Games offer all of the world's nations a taste of harmony and coexistence for the brief period they are in session.

For all of these reasons, world-class athletes such as Roger Federer set their sights on the Olympics. Federer's first quest for an Olympic medal began on September 15, 2000, when he attended the Games in Sydney, Australia. Federer was nineteen years old, in his second year as a professional tennis player, and ranked number thirty-six in the world. His prospects for a medal looked good.

# The Olympic Tradition

The modern Olympic Games were first held in 1896 in Athens, Greece. The competitions lasted ten days and included the sports of cycling, fencing, gymnastics, shooting, swimming, tennis, weight lifting, and wrestling. A number of events that are now categorized as track and field sports were also included. Fourteen countries sent athletes to compete in the various sporting contests.

Since then the Olympics have been held every four years and have taken place in a different country each year. The Games have been held on schedule with the exception of the ones in 1916, which were canceled due to World War I, and those in 1940 and 1944, which were canceled as a result of World War II.

*The Panathinaiko Stadium, shown here, hosted the first modern Olympics in 1896 in Athens, Greece.*

# A Bumpy Ride for Federer in Sydney

Federer's 2000 Olympic journey got off to a rough start. The Swiss tennis team was falling apart. Both of the Swiss women, Martina Hingis and her doubles partner, Patty Schnyder, withdrew from competition. Hingis withdrew less than two weeks before the opening ceremonies, citing a heavy competition schedule and fear of injury.

The third member of the Swiss tennis team, Marc Rosset, also withdrew from the Olympics shortly before the start of the Games. He stated that he was mentally and physically exhausted and not in condition to play. As a result, Federer was the only tennis player who represented Switzerland. He lost his chance to play in men's doubles, since Rosset was to be his partner, but was hopeful for success in men's singles.

Federer excelled in singles, finishing with better standings than expected. He won his first four matches, placing him in the semifinal competition and within reach of an Olympic medal. He played cautiously and lost to German Tommy Haas, however, which eliminated the possibility of a gold or silver medal. He did qualify for the bronze medal match, in which he played against Arnaud Di Pasquale of France. Federer lost the match, however, and received no medal. The loss was a major disappointment, and he was visibly upset. "Considering how the match was going, I should never have lost," he said. "I really wanted to be standing on the podium. Now I have nothing to take home except my pride."[30]

Yet Federer thoroughly enjoyed his Olympic experience, beginning with the spectacular opening ceremony. He became friends with many other athletes during his stay in the Olympic Village (a set of dormitories reserved for athletes and coaches) By the end of the Games, he was spending time with someone special—female tennis player Mirka Vavrinec, a native of the Czech Republic. As they parted ways after the conclusion of the Olympics, romance followed them. Several months later, reporters leaked the news that the couple was dating.

## Another Try for Gold in Athens

In August 2004 the Olympics took place in their original home of Athens, Greece. Federer again was placed on the Swiss Olympic tennis team. He was accompanied by doubles partner Yves Allegro, his former roommate and good friend. The Swiss women's team consisted of Patty Schnyder and Myriam Casanova. The four athletes formed a solid team compared to the one in 2000.

The Games got off to a great start for Federer. By this time he had won Wimbledon twice and was the number one ranked tennis player in the world. This placed him as the number one seed

*Federer returning a shot against Nikolay Davydenko in the 2004 Olympic Games in Athens. He beat Davydenko but later lost to Tomáš Berdych of the Czech Republic.*

in the Olympic lineup—the top-ranked player. At the opening ceremony for the Games, he was given the honor of carrying the Swiss flag for his team. Federer was optimistic about his prospects for a medal.

The Athens Games soon became tarnished for the Swiss tennis team, however. Casanova lost in her first round of singles play, and Schnyder lost in her third round. In doubles the pair was defeated in the second round.

The men found themselves facing a similar fate. Federer and Allegro lost in the second round of men's doubles, and Allegro did not play in men's singles. Federer won his first round against Nikolay Davydenko of Russia but suffered a shocking defeat in his match against Tomáš Berdych of the Czech Republic, who was ranked far below him at number seventy-nine.

Federer was surprised and discouraged by the loss. "It's a terrible day for me, you know, losing singles and doubles. Obviously I was aiming for a better result than this, but that's what I got. So I have to live with it." Referring to his heavy tournament schedule leading up to the Olympics, he said, "I've been playing non-stop, you know. ... And it's obvious it's going to catch up with me, eventually. ... Unfortunately it's during the Olympics."[31]

## New Hope in Beijing

Federer traveled to Beijing, China, in 2008 for his third Olympics. The stakes were high: It would probably be his last chance for gold. The next Olympic opportunity would not come along until the 2012 Olympic Games. He would be approaching his thirty-first birthday by that time, and he could not predict whether he would still be in peak physical condition to consider another try. In all likelihood 2008 would be his last real chance to win an Olympic medal.

The year got off to a rough start for Federer. He had no wins early in the year and then was diagnosed with mononucleosis, which required him to take time off to recover and regain his strength. But the 2008 Summer Olympics started out full of promise for Federer. The opening ceremony was held on August

# The Modern Summer and Winter Games

In 1924 the Olympic Games were expanded into two separate competitions. The existing Olympics was deemed the Summer Games, and a separate competition was established to feature sports played on snow or ice. The first Olympic Winter Games were held in 1924 in Chamonix, France. The Winter and Summer Olympics were held in the same year, every four years, until 1992, when the International Olympic Committee decided the events would be better if they were not squeezed into the same year. The competitions now alternate every two years.

The Summer Olympics currently feature events in forty-four sporting categories. Hundreds of distinct events take place, since each sport is divided into a number of competitions. Swimming, for example, consists of thirty-four separate races for men, women, and teams. Tennis is broken into four events: men's singles and doubles, and women's singles and doubles. Events have been added or removed from competition throughout the history of the Olympics. Tennis, in fact, was dropped as an Olympic sport in 1928 because of conflicts with the Wimbledon tennis competition and disagreements about Olympic tennis rules. The sport returned to the Olympic Games in 1988.

8—Federer's twenty-seventh birthday. As in the previous Olympics, he was again chosen as Switzerland's flag bearer and led his team of eighty-four athletes into the Olympic Stadium. His tennis teammates were Stanislas Wawrinka, who was Federer's doubles partner, plus Patty Schnyder, Emmanuelle Gagliardi, and Timea Bacsinszky. Federer expressed his excitement about the opening of the Games: "This is very special. I'm thrilled it's the Opening Ceremony on my birthday and I get to carry the flag for Switzerland. And, obviously, you can imagine what that means to me."[32]

## Pressure and Demands on the Tennis Star

Unlike his previous two Olympics, Federer opted to stay in a hotel rather than in the Olympic Village. Although he enjoyed the constant activity of the Village and the interaction with other athletes, he chose peace and privacy instead. He wanted to avoid the many reporters and photographers and also to be free to come and go according to his own schedule in a quieter setting. As Federer explained to an interviewer: "There is too much attention, including from other athletes. I want to prepare perfectly so that means getting away from it."[33]

Indeed, Federer had much to escape from. He had already received considerable publicity after being placed on the Swiss Olympic team. In addition to standard announcements by Switzerland's Olympic Committee, reporters quizzed him about

*Due to the considerable attention Federer received from reporters, athletes, and the general public, he opted to stay in a hotel rather than the Olympic village for the 2008 Beijing Olympics.*

his expectations for the Games in the weeks leading up to the event. Interest in Federer was multiplied by his appearance in a promotional video created by the International Olympic Committee. The commercial featured a robust, gray-bearded man with a deep voice welcoming and recognizing popular athletes at a mythical competition in a columned pavilion similar to a Greek temple. It played up the superhuman abilities of the athletes as a way of stirring interest in the Olympics. Federer was depicted swatting a fireball with his tennis racket. The commercial's narrator described him as "the Invincible Man—you teach us to give up our best no matter how great the pressure."[34] The video also featured Chinese basketball player Yao Ming, Swedish track athlete Carolina Klüft, Chinese runner Liu Xiang, Russian pole vaulter Yelena Isinbaeva, and several others.

## Federer Battles on the Olympic Courts

On the second day of the Olympic competition, the men's tennis matches got underway. Federer, who was the top-seeded player, won his first match against Dmitry Tursunov of Russia. Reporter David Cox of the website Tennistalk.com noted: "Tursunov was no match [for Federer] today. ... This match clearly meant a lot to Federer. ... [He] appeared in top shape."[35]

Federer also won in the second round of play against Rafael Arevalo of El Salvador. That moved him ahead to the third round, in which he faced Tomáš Berdych of the Czech Republic. Berdych had beaten Federer at the Athens Olympics in 2004, ending his dream of a medal that year. This time, though, Federer prevailed and won the round. The quarterfinal round was next, placing him just two games away from an Olympic medal, but Federer would again see his dream evaporate. In a hard-fought game following a long rain delay, American James Blake defeated Federer.

The Olympics had not been any kinder to the rest of the Swiss tennis players. Stanislas Wawrinka won his first match against Canadian Frank Dancevic but was defeated in the second round of play by Jurgen Melzer of Austria. In doubles play, Emmanuelle Gagliardi

# Tennis Courts

**T**ennis matches are played on grass, clay, or hard courts. Each surface has advantages and disadvantages. Top-ranked tennis players must be versatile enough to overcome the challenges of each type.

Grass courts resemble a backyard lawn, but the grass is trimmed short and the soil is packed hard. Players must overcome the drag caused by the grass and underlying soil. Games on grass are faster than on clay courts or hard courts, but balls do not bounce very high. Wimbledon matches are played on grass.

Clay courts have a reddish-orange or green appearance. They are made of natural clay or crushed bricks mixed with rubber and other materials. Games on clay are slower than on grass or hard courts. Balls bounce slower but higher and more predictably. Clay courts can be slippery and can cause problems for footwork, and players usually get covered in dust. The French Open uses clay courts.

Hard courts are typically made of asphalt or a high-tech blend of materials including rubber. Games on a hard court are faster than clay but slower than grass. Hard courts cause the fewest problems for footwork, and games tend to be fast because of the speed and height of ball bounces. Games at the Australian Open and U.S. Open are played on hard courts.

and Patty Schnyder easily won their first round against the Greek team but were eliminated in their second round by the team from China. In singles Timea Bacsinszky lost her first round, and Patty Schnyder advanced to the second round, where she was defeated.

## A Final Chance for the Men in Doubles

The last hope for the Swiss tennis team lay in the men's doubles. In the first round of play, Federer and Wawrinka easily defeated

*Roger Federer (left) and Stanislas Wawrinka of Switzerland win gold against Thomas Johansson and Simon Aspelin of Sweden during the men's doubles match at the Olympic Green Tennis Center on Day 8 of the Beijing 2008 Olympic Games.*

the Italian team. The second round brought another easy victory against the Russian players. The Swiss men advanced to the quarterfinal—only two games away from a chance for a medal. They faced the pair from India and seized another victory, moving them into the semifinal round. A win in the semifinal would mean placement in the final game to determine the gold and silver medals; a loss would place them in the game for a bronze medal—or no medal at all.

Federer and Wawrinka, the fourth-ranked team, faced top-seeded American brothers Bob and Mike Bryan. The Swiss men prevailed, moving them into the battle for a gold medal. This win guaranteed that Federer and Wawrinka would finish with no less than a silver medal.

The final tennis game of the 2008 Olympics pitted Federer and Wawrinka against Swedes Simon Aspelin and Thomas Johansson. The pairs were more evenly matched than in earlier games, but the Swiss men dominated and won the gold medal. After the final point, Federer and Wawrinka hugged and hopped around on the court. Wawrinka flopped down on the asphalt as if overcome by exhaustion, and Federer laid his hands on his partner's chest and then floated them over his body as if checking to see that he was alive and all right. The men hugged and rolled on the court as a videographer closed in to capture their winning moment.

The two were thrilled. "It is like a fantastic dream comes true, I feel really happy to win the gold medal," Federer told interviewers. "I have tried for several times (to get a medal), and I came really close to the medal in Sydney where I finished fourth. ... It is really special also because it is for Switzerland."[36]

The pair stood atop the podium proudly as they received their red-ribboned gold medals and bouquets of red roses, smiling and waving to the crowd. Federer's emotion was visible on his face as the Swiss flag was raised and the Swiss national anthem was played. His eight-year pursuit of an Olympic medal had been rewarded, and he had seized the only major tennis prize that had remained missing from his impressive collection of awards.

# Chapter 4

# Behind the Scenes

To his fans and the public, Roger Federer's life appears to take place entirely on tennis courts, in press conferences, and frequently, accepting a trophy. His life, though, is not as straightforward as showing up at the court, playing a match, and going home with pockets stuffed with prize money. Off camera he is besieged by the demands of training, traveling, tending to finances and corporate sponsors, and working with agents, managers, and coaches. In the midst of all these obligations, he tries to find time for family and friends.

Federer is constantly busy with tasks of which most fans are probably unaware. "I think a lot of people don't quite understand what it takes to be No. 1," he told legendary tennis player Billie Jean King. "I've got so many commitments—you have the sponsors, the TV, the radio, the newspapers, your own charity, other charities. ... Also you've got to work—conditioning, practicing."[37] Federer would probably be the first to agree that juggling his career with his personal life requires constant work and attention.

## Trainings and Practices

Federer's main priority is his success on the court. In order to stay healthy and avoid injuries, he eats a healthy diet, participates in conditioning and strength training, and of course, relentlessly practices his game. Even at the age of fourteen, he practiced five

*Roger Federer takes time off the court to sign an auto-graph.*

to six hours per week, worked at conditioning training two to three hours a week, and took part in tournaments two or three times per month. As a professional, he practices and trains almost every day. His former trainer, Paul Dorochenko, says Federer's perseverance has paid off. "There is no success without hard work. He invested a lot of his preparation in coordination, strength and physical fitness."[38] Since turning pro, Federer has been known to exhaust his coaches in trainings and warm-ups.

Federer's training schedule changes continuously. It often depends upon the time of year and the ATP schedule, upcoming tournaments and the type of court, any physical weaknesses or problems he is experiencing, and other commitments that might get in the way of training. Typically, when at home, he plays on the court and works out for about four hours a day. During tournaments, he works out less often, instead reserving his energy for his matches.

Federer's workout regimen consists of activities meant to improve agility, endurance, and speed. His workouts typically include sprints and interval training, which involves bursts of high intensity movement. He also stretches and lifts weights.

"I like lifting weights," he says, and notes that his workout is defined by a variety of exercises and moves. "Tennis players do a lot of different kinds of exercises—gym, muscle training, sprints; footwork, coordination. I like to mix it up."[39]

Federer is kept in top shape by his fitness trainer, Pierre Paganini. He designs fitness routines that include running, weights, and a variety of exercises engineered to keep Federer at his peak of speed, agility, and strength. They frequently toss a large, weighted ball called a medicine ball over the net on the tennis court. Before major tournaments, they might work out as many as ten hours per week.

Before matches, Federer always makes sure to stretch and warm up. In fact, prematch stretching and warm-ups have become increasingly important to him. When he was younger, he was lazy about this; he preferred to play video games until it was time for his matches. As he got older, however, he became more disciplined about warm-ups because they help him prepare for his strenuous games. When asked by an interviewer how he avoids injuries, he said: "You've just got to warm up very well, make sure you do the exercises, take extra time for treatment [massages] before and after, that kind of thing. ... I made sure I did all the right things."[40]

## Balancing Work and Rest

Federer also maintains his peak condition by making sure he gets enough sleep. "Sleeping is very important for me. Otherwise, I hurt myself," he told interviewer Felix Latzer. "When I'm tired, I plug my ears and sleep."[41]

Sometimes, being a well-rested tennis pro means missing out on some fun. When Federer and his girlfriend attended a charity event the night before the first round of Wimbledon, for example, the couple departed promptly at 11:00 P.M. so the tennis champ could get his rest. Although the evening's entertainment was just getting started, the couple understood that sleep was a priority if Federer was to play well the next day.

In addition to being well-rested, Federer takes care not to over-

*Federer poses for a photo with his mother, Lynette, and father, Robert, as they arrive at the Wimbledon Winners Dinner in 2005.*

work his body. Massage is among his many training secrets: He relies on a personal massage therapist to help him cope with minor problems such as sprains, bruises, muscle pulls, sore joints, and aches. Federer also credits regular massages with keeping him flexible and helping him avoid injuries by preparing his muscles for the rigors of tennis matches. His massage therapist is present during tournaments and can be called on quickly if needed.

To stay mentally healthy, Federer also takes time to unwind, sometimes by playing video games. He is a big fan of the PlayStation video game console and occasionally uses it to pass the time while waiting for tennis matches to start and as a release from hectic activity. When asked about the games he likes to play, he said that he enjoys the tennis games very much. "I like the way Rafa [Rafael Nadal] and [Gaël] Monfils play. But of course I also enjoy playing against myself!"[42]

Like most people, Federer also relaxes by spending time with friends and family. When asked by a reporter about his off-duty time during tournaments, he talked about habits that help him unwind. "[I] take it easy. Have nice dinners and lunches. I have some treatment, massage, stretches, hang out with my friends and family."[43]

## The Business of a Tennis Star

Handling Federer's tournament schedule, personal appearances, interview requests, and travel is more than a full-time job. He attends fifteen to twenty tournaments around the globe every year and makes other appearances as well. Since 2005 he has depended upon American Tony Godsick, a professional sports manager, to handle business matters such as contracts and finances. Godsick accompanies Federer to nearly all of his tournaments to manage publicity, media, and any sudden needs.

Despite the assistance of his manager and his lawyers, Federer stays involved in all of the decisions regarding his finances and career. Celebrities and athletes have sometimes been swindled out of great amounts of money or have lost money because of poor decision making by their managers. Federer has been cau-

# Federer Merchandise

Roger Federer has a successful sideline business with his own line of clothes and accessories. His items bear his unique RF logo and include T-shirts, caps and visors, calendars, a handbag, jigsaw puzzle, and autographed items. Purchases support Federer's charity. His online store, found on his website, also includes links to Nike and Wilson and his specialty items on those sites. Federer believes that his logo and merchandise allow fans to make a connection to him and show their support for his career.

tious to avoid suffering that fate. "I approve everything," he told a *New York Times* reporter. "You see and hear that [an athlete has lost his fortune] and always wish that it's not going to happen to you, but you hardly ever have a guarantee, except, of course, if you really take it into your own hands like I did."[44]

## A Family Man

While some celebrities keep their families in the background of their lives, Federer's family gets a front row seat. He keeps his family close in part because he believes he could not have achieved his success without their help. He is particularly grateful to his parents. "They invested an enormous amount of time and also a lot of money when I was young to allow me to play tennis," he says on his website. "I have always had wonderful support from them."[45]

Robert and Lynette Federer not only helped their son launch his career—they still assist him with travel arrangements and help answer fan mail and coordinate with some of his fan clubs. Lynette also has an active role in his charity, the Roger Federer Foundation. The Federers are frequently seen at their son's tennis tournaments, engrossed in the action, and have even made a cameo appearance in a humorous commercial for Jura coffee makers in which Roger takes a coffee break in midgame.

Federer's commitment to family deepened when he married his longtime girlfriend, Mirka Vavrinec, on April 11, 2009, after nine years of dating. He happily posted news of the wedding on his website. The couple enjoyed a small gathering with close friends and family in Basel on a beautiful spring Sunday. Mirka is her husband's most enthusiastic fan, constant companion, and personal aide. She is also his business partner. She arranges his travel and accommodations, schedules interview requests, and works with the manager of his website. Federer described Mirka's importance to his professional and personal life: "I think the tennis life can be sometimes a very lonely life. You know, you're just there and you know you're waiting for your matches. And there's a lot of waiting going on for us in the business. You know,

*Federer's wife Mirka is his biggest fan, as well as his business partner and personal aide. In 2009 the pair welcomed twins into their family.*

if Mirka is there, we're having a good time all of us together. I never feel like I'm lonely. I never feel like the life is boring."[46]

Federer's family grew on July 23, 2009, when he and Mirka became the parents of twin girls, Myla Rose and Charlene Riva. When asked about fatherhood, he told a reporter: "We love our role and try to be the best parents we can. It's definitely a very positive change in my life. I didn't expect that, but it's a pleasant surprise. We're enjoying every second with them."[47]

## Friendly Support for the Tennis Hero

In addition to his family, Federer depends upon several close friends. Federer counts Reto Staubli, a former national tennis player for Switzerland, as a close friend and confidante. Staubli was Federer's best man at his wedding and has traveled extensively to be at Federer's side during major matches. Federer credits Staubli as aiding him during some major decisions in his life, such as changing coaches. Other close friends in the tennis world include Yves Allegro, Marco Chiudinelli, and Severin Lüthi.

Federer is also good friends with music stars Gavin Rossdale and Gwen Stefani. Rossdale, a tennis fan, and Federer, a fan of

Rossdale's band Bush, met many years ago and have been close friends ever since. Rossdale and Stefani have cheered for Federer from his reserved seats on the tennis court at Wimbledon as well as at many tournaments in the United States.

Federer considers his coaches to be part of his circle of friends. He is especially close to Peter Lundgren, Tony Roche, Severin Lüthi, and Paul Annacone. He is on good terms with José Higueras, a coach who specializes in clay court surfaces. Higueras helped Federer improve his performance at tournaments that use clay courts, such as the French Open.

## Sponsors and Endorsements

Like many athletes, Federer has several corporate sponsors that pay him to advertise their products. His endorsement contracts add up to millions of dollars of income every year.

Within Switzerland, Federer works with the investment banking firm Credit Suisse, which features Federer on its corporate website. Nationale Suisse, another financial company, also sponsors Federer and features him in a commercial. The Lindt chocolate company is another corporation that has formed a rela-

## Measures of Greatness

Roger Federer has been the recipient of many awards over his career that reflect his good manners, positive image, and charitable efforts. These include: ESPY Best Male Tennis Player (2005–2010); Fan's Favorite, ATPWorldTour.com (2003–2010); ATPWorldTour.com Player of the Decade (2009); ITF Player of the Year (2004, 2007, 2009); Stefan Edberg Sportsmanship Award (2004–2009); Laureus World Sportsman of the Year (2005–2008); Swiss Athlete of the Year (2003, 2004, 2006, 2007); Arthur Ashe Humanitarian of the Year (2006); Sports Illustrated Tennis Player of the Year (2004); and Swiss of the Year (2003).

tionship with Federer. The Lindt website proudly describes the partnership: "With his likeable and down to earth image, Federer is the ideal brand ambassador. ... He uniquely embodies Lindt & Sprungli's fundamental values of 'Swissness,' 'Premiumness,' 'Quality' and 'Passion.' ... The names of Lindt and Federer symbolizes the perfect 'match' between the number 1 in premium chocolate and the number 1 in the world of tennis."[48] Federer also appears in magazine ads and television commercials for Jura, another Swiss company, which makes high-quality coffee and espresso machines.

Federer has several big-name brand endorsements outside of Switzerland as well. One is Gillette razors, which supplies him with razors and skin care products; in exchange, he is required always to look well groomed and clean shaven. Another spon-

*The Nike tennis shoes of Roger Federer during a match on day two of the Wimbledon 2011 Championships. Nike is one of Federer's most visible corporate sponsers.*

# A Reluctant Publicity Magnet

**A** large part of Roger Federer's career involves dealing with the media. He frequently faces reporters, interviews, and press conferences. These typically take place after tournaments, and Federer is peppered with questions from journalists.

Federer admitted that for a long time, he would have liked to avoid reporters and interviews. Speaking in public made him nervous, but he eventually got better at it. "Initially I didn't enjoy awards presentations and walking the red carpet and all that stuff. And usually when I had to make a speech, it really freaked me out. ... I still get nervous when I have to give a speech. I think it helps you to face fear so you can move on."

Quoted in Billie Jean King. "Roger Federer." *Interview*, July 2006, p. 66.

sor is Mercedes-Benz automobiles; Federer drives a bright red Mercedes-Benz SLS AMG gull-wing supercar valued at about two hundred thousand dollars. Rolex watches also sponsors the tennis star. Federer's website shows a Rolex watch face that keeps real time, displaying the correct time of his location, whether at home or at any tournament he is playing. Another sponsor is the private airline NetJets, which offers personalized air travel.

Federer's most visible sponsors are Nike apparel and Wilson tennis equipment. His arrangement with Nike provides him with a steady supply of shoes, socks, and clothing, which he wears in all tennis matches. Nike's website includes a Roger Federer specialty line of shoes, shirts, shorts, and caps.

Wilson athletic equipment features a profile of Federer on its website, describes his tennis racket in detail, and offers merchandise bearing Federer's photo and simulated signature, such as gear bags. His racket is the Wilson Six.One Tour BLX, which the company supplies to him. He uses about sixty frames per year;

the frames are restrung as needed, for a total of six hundred to seven hundred restrings per year. At any given time, Federer has about one hundred tennis rackets and fifty pairs of shoes at home.

## Print Ads and Television Commercials

Sponsors often ask celebrities to appear in commercials, which can be fun or sometimes stressful. Federer seems to enjoy his photo shoots and commercial sessions. His website includes a gallery of his sponsors, samples of his commercials, and some outtakes from his video shoots. Appearing in commercials is sometimes more difficult than it looks. In preparing for a commercial for Wilson tennis rackets, for example, the director asked him to work on his pronunciation of the word *this* to make it sound more American. With his German accent, it often sounded like *dis* or *zhis*. He repeated the line "How does this make you feel?" many times and attempted the word *this* at least sixteen times. Federer was good-natured about getting the line right, but the video reveals that commercials often take a lot of preparation.

In a separate photo shoot for Gillette razors, Federer goofed around between shots. He asked an assistant to balance an aluminum water bottle on his head, then smacked a tennis ball at the bottle, knocking it off perfectly. To prove it was not luck, he set up the shot again, and hit the bottle squarely a second time. The lighthearted moment shows that he is quite at ease while filming commercials.

Federer enjoys photo sessions and commercial shoots because they give him a break from tennis. "I take great pleasure in doing photo shoots or films [commercials] sometimes, just because it's so different to my everyday life as a tennis player," he said.[49] For him, such projects are one of many aspects of his life that represent his hard work and success and his dreams coming true.

# Chapter 5

# Tennis Star and Humanitarian

As a professional athlete, much of Roger Federer's life occurs in public for the whole world to see. Whether he has a bad day or a good day, slips up in an interview, or performs an act of kindness, any of his public moments might be caught on video, recorded forever, and viewed on the Internet an infinite number of times. Yet even with this constant scrutiny, he has maintained a solid image as a kind, considerate, upstanding tennis player and human being. He has never been caught in a scandal or gossiping about other players. Instead, he is polite, levelheaded, and patient in public. He has participated in many charitable efforts and has donated large sums of money through his personal charity.

## The Charitable Gentleman

Since turning professional in 1999, media experts have estimated that Federer has won about $62 million in prize money. He receives another $30 million to $40 million each year in endorsement income. With so much money at his disposal, Federer realized early in his career that he could make a difference in the lives of others. He explained: "As a player you get many requests for

*Roger Federer is presented a check by Ralf Weber for his foundation after his match against Rohan Bopanna of India.*

charity—people want your name, a racket, clothes. They want you to attend an event, and it makes you wonder. So I decided I was going to do something myself."[50] He became determined to make charitable efforts a large focus of his life and his wealth.

After Federer won his first Wimbledon title, which came with a prize of about £500,000 (about U.S. $800,000), he felt he was in a good position to start his own charitable foundation. He launched the Roger Federer Foundation in late 2003, when he was twenty-two years old. He told Billie Jean King, who asked him about starting the charity at such a young age: "I remember hearing [American tennis player] Andre [Agassi] say once he wished he had started [his charity] earlier. So I said, 'Let's get it going and do as much as we can now. I know this is the prime of my career. … Let's get it underway … and try to help more and more people.'"[51]

Federer's parents and Mirka (who was his girlfriend at that time) were enthusiastic. His mother remembered, "At the end of 2003, when Roger was having great success in tennis, we discussed [forming a foundation] within the management because we felt that he wanted to give something back."[52] The Roger Federer Foundation was formed and made its first donations within a few months.

## Designing a Plan for a Good Cause

South Africa seemed like a natural choice for his charity to reach out, since it was Lynette Federer's homeland and many people there lived in poverty. Federer had visited South Africa many times in his life. It seemed like a good place to start using his fortune to help disadvantaged children.

The Federer family first worked with the Imbewu organization, which had connections in Switzerland. This agency's mission was to provide relief to children in the city of Port Elizabeth, South Africa—specifically, in the New Brighton township. This township was recognized as one of the poorest and most overcrowded slums in South Africa. Almost every day, the residents see death from disease, AIDS, and violence.

Federer's foundation gradually took shape. His family decided to direct its efforts toward education for impoverished children in South Africa as well as promoting youth sports for children in Switzerland. In 2003 the Roger Federer Foundation began providing money for books, uniforms, supplies, and other needs that enabled approximately sixty New Brighton children to attend school each year. It also gave access to sports programs and provided special help with family problems for about 250 children in Port Elizabeth.

## A Journey with a Purpose

In early 2005 Federer flew to Port Elizabeth to visit the areas targeted for his contributions. Someone close to him suggested that he take along a media crew to record his trip and use the footage for publicity, but he did not like the idea. He had no desire to make his efforts public and felt that fulfilling his purpose was satisfaction enough.

Federer was joined on the trip by his mother, his girlfriend, and a woman from the ATP. She convinced him to bring a photographer and cameraman and to invite a local journalist in order to have a personal record of the trip.

The visit was spent meeting children and families, playing ball, handing out T-shirts, and getting a feel for the township. Federer enjoyed the trip and was pleased to see how his foundation could impact the families in the area. Late in 2005 the Federer family donated a sports facility to New Brighton township suitable for soccer, basketball, and netball. His mother described the family's philosophy about their donations: "With a small project you have a better overview of what's happening. You know all the people working there and you can really see the improvements among the children and the community."[53]

## New Hope for Forgotten Children

As Federer's bank account grew, his foundation was able to expand its reach. He became aware that girls in underdeveloped countries faced a special set of problems. They were less likely to attend school than boys. Their lack of schooling not only held them back later in life, but it also made them less able to cope with problems such as violence and put them less in control of their own lives. The foundation turned its attention to Ethiopia, Malawi, Mali, and Zimbabwe, helping about eight thousand children—among them a high percentage of girls—to attend school.

One of the students who was able to attend school with the help of the foundation made an unexpected impact on Federer and his charity. The fifteen-year-old girl named Nolonwabo Batini, from Ndzondelelo High School in Port Elizabeth, South Africa, made the simple statement, "I am tomorrow's future."[54] Her words moved Federer and his family so much that they have become part of the charity's mission. Her quote appears in several places on the foundation's website and is used to help steer the direction of charitable efforts.

*Roger Federer poses with local schoolchildren during his visit to a school funded by the Roger Federer Foundation in Kore Roba, Ethiopia.*

## Giving Back to His Homeland

At home in Switzerland, the Federer family looked for ways to help aspiring young athletes. They chose to sponsor individual children in the age group of eleven to eighteen by providing scholarships for their athletic training costs. Because Federer had the benefit of sponsors in his youth, this felt like an appropriate way to pass along his good fortune. Each year, his foundation enables twenty-four young athletes to pursue their dreams in their chosen sports.

Most of the money that the foundation uses for its selected projects comes from Federer's earnings. Some of it also comes from donations and merchandise sales in his online shop. On his website he explains his mission and thanks his fans who support his cause.

> It is important to me to give back some of the luck that I am able to experience in my life. I have chosen to help children in the poorest regions of our world by means of my Foundation. If we can combine our efforts we can reach even higher goals. So I want to thank you. ... By purchasing these articles you are making a direct contribution towards making our planet a better place for the youngest ones of our society.[55]

## Putting the "Fun" in Fund-Raising

Federer has also become known as a driving force in the world of celebrity sporting events for charity. He has organized a number of tennis matches to raise money for natural disasters, such as the 2010 earthquake in Haiti and the 2010–2011 floods in Queensland, Australia. By recruiting fellow tennis players to donate their time and play in special charity matches, he has been able to draw huge, paying crowds to watch these events, with the proceeds going directly to disaster relief.

During the Australian Open in January 2010, for example, he organized Hit for Haiti on short notice. The event was a series of exhibition tennis matches among the biggest names in tennis. Profits from the event went directly to victims of the earthquake that had devastated Haiti earlier that same month. *Sports Illustrated* magazine called it "an impromptu exhibition that represented everything right about tennis."[56] The magazine reported that the event sold out the Rod Laver Arena, raised millions of dollars, and brought attention to the tremendous amount of work that needed to be done to restore the country.

The event was so successful that Hit for Haiti 2 followed in March 2010. This exhibition event was organized during the BNP Paribas Open at Indian Wells, California. The owner of the tournament, Larry Ellison, promoted the benefit event. It included a

*Former tennis player Pete Sampras and Roger Federer having a good time during Hit for Haiti 2, a charity event during the BNP Paribas Open on March 12, 2010, in Indian Wells, California.*

doubles match among four major tennis legends: Roger Federer and Pete Sampras played against Rafael Nadal and Andre Agassi. The event raised another $1 million for disaster relief in Haiti.

In 2011 Federer spearheaded a similar benefit called Rally for Relief, with proceeds going to help victims of flooding in Queensland, Australia. Some of tennis's top players, including Rafael Nadal, took part. The event was not merely a string of tennis matches, but a long series of games designed for entertainment. Players wore microphones and teased each other, as well as the line judges, during the games. They also fooled around with trick shots and risky, flamboyant moves just to dazzle the crowd. Reporter Darren Saligari of the Australian Open website

# Andre Agassi

**A**ndre Agassi is credited as one of the greatest tennis players in the history of the game. He turned professional at age sixteen and was ranked number one in the world at age twenty-five, in April 1995. Agassi held the number one title for thirty weeks, until November 1995.

Agassi has stood out in the world of tennis for more than just his accomplishments on the court. His hairstyle has been the subject of much discussion. In the 1990s Agassi's hair was long and spiky, giving him a look more like a rock star than a polished professional tennis player. He eventually cut his hair and shaved his head, giving him a more clean-cut look, but an earring helped him retain his tough-guy appearance.

Roger Federer credits Agassi for inspiring him to start his charitable foundation at a young age. Agassi started his own charity in 1994 with the purpose of helping underprivileged children and youth in the Las Vegas area. Today Agassi is recognized as one of the most charitable players in tennis.

*Andre Agassi plays in an exhibition match at the 2009 Roland Garros tournament.*

compared it to a Harlem Globetrotters game on a tennis court. The event brought in more than $1.5 million for flood victims.

## Rivals on the Court, Friends in the Real World

Sports competitors are often thought of as rivals or even enemies, but Federer says he rarely feels this way about other tennis players. He separates his feelings about tennis matches from his feelings about the players. When games or tournaments do not go his way, he does not blame the other players. After a loss, he is often heard in press conferences complimenting his opponent and sometimes critiquing his own game. He often admits that an opponent deserved to win because of superior play or that he deserved to lose because his game was off.

Federer's well-balanced attitude helps him to keep a cool head and makes him well liked by other tennis players. This is important, because they often compete against good friends. Federer, for example, has played professionally against his longtime friend Marco Chiudinelli, his former roommate Yves Allegro, and his former Olympic doubles partner Stanislas Wawrinka. In 2011 at the BNP Paribas Open in California, he defeated Wawrinka in singles in the quarterfinal round, but Wawrinka was Federer's doubles partner in the very same tournament.

The man whom most people consider Federer's biggest rival, Rafael Nadal, is in fact one of Federer's closest tennis friends. The two share a warm relationship on the tennis court and are sometimes seen together during their free time. Nadal took over the number one ranking in tennis from Federer in August 2008, but Federer won it back in July 2009. Nadal again took the spot from Federer in June 2010. Sports analysts continually spoke of the Federer-Nadal rivalry, but from all appearances, the rivalry exists for everyone in the tennis world except the two players.

This was evident in the charity match Federer organized with Nadal in December 2010. At the time, Nadal was ranked number one and Federer number two, and the two men teamed up to earn money for their personal charities. Federer and Nadal played each other in Zurich, Switzerland, in what was called Match for Africa. The event raised $2.6 million for the Roger Federer Foundation, and Federer won the match in his home country. The very next evening the men played a similar tournament in Madrid, Spain, called Joining Forces for the Benefit of Children. It collected $1.3 million for Nadal's own charity. Nadal won the event before his fans in his native Spain.

Federer is also quick to help his friends with their own charitable causes. He has appeared many times at celebrity tennis matches and also at benefit events such as Elton John's AIDS foundation. His friend Yves Allegro described Federer's generous nature when he revealed:

> He's a very solid person. Once I had asked him to play an exhibition event at the club, he gave me the dates three months in advance and stuck to them even after he won Wimbledon (in 2003). He played for free. 3000 people turned up for the game when the population of the town was only 2000! It just goes to show his character.[57]

## Honored by UNICEF

In 2006 Federer received the honor of being appointed an international goodwill ambassador for the United Nations International Children's Emergency Fund, better known as UNICEF. The charity frequently invites celebrities of good character to travel to impoverished countries and see the work that UNICEF is accomplishing. Afterward, they report to the public about the situations they witness. They often appear at fund-raisers and on television to spread the message about the needs of children throughout the world. Past international goodwill ambassadors have included soccer star David Beckham, actor Orlando Bloom, and actress-comedianne Whoopi Goldberg.

Federer was pleased by the opportunity. At a press conference announcing his new role, he said: "I may have achieved a lot on the court, but I would also like to try to achieve more now off

*Roger Federer (L) gets a UNICEF pin from UNICEF Executive Director Ann M. Veneman after Federer was named as a Goodwill Ambassador on April 3, 2006 in New York City.*

the court. That's one of my big goals in the future, and it's really a privilege for me to continue this great tradition of UNICEF."[58]

UNICEF executive director Ann M. Veneman noted that Federer's charitable nature was the reason he was selected for the position.

> Talent is not the only thing that sets Roger Federer apart from the rest of the sports world. Our interest in appointing him as a Goodwill Ambassador was inspired by his personal story and the commitment he has demonstrated to using his fame to benefit children.[59]

The relationship between UNICEF and Federer began in 2005 when he made a large personal donation to UNICEF's relief

# UNICEF

In 1946, after the end of World War II had left millions of children displaced or orphaned, the United Nations General Assembly established the United Nations International Children's Emergency Fund, more commonly called UNICEF. The goal was to provide food, clothing, shelter, and necessities to children in need throughout the world.

Since that time, the program has accepted millions of dollars in donations and has funneled aid to children all over the world. It has also started vaccination programs to help prevent deaths from the spread of disease. The program eventually expanded from emergency relief to daily assistance in poverty-stricken countries. UNICEF also helps to provide medical care to children and pregnant women.

For many years the organization has spread its message through national and international goodwill ambassadors such as Roger Federer. These individuals are selected for their standout character and humanitarian interests. They travel to foreign countries to witness UNICEF's services firsthand, then make appearances to spread the word about UNICEF and assist in encouraging donations.

efforts following the Indian Ocean tsunami and then organized one of his first celebrity tennis matches for that cause. That event also formed a permanent bond between UNICEF and the ATP.

With all of Federer's success, recognition, and charitable efforts, he could easily become demanding, difficult to work with, or arrogant. Yet in public appearances, tennis matches, and off court, he is almost always pleasant and modest. On the Roger Federer Foundation website, he describes his philosophy about keeping a positive attitude: "It's nice to be important, but it's more important to be nice."[60]

# Chapter 6

# Still Swinging

At the beginning of 2005, Roger Federer was exactly where he wanted to be. He was number one in the ATP world rankings. He had won Wimbledon, his dream since childhood, not just once, but twice. He had also won two other Grand Slam titles at the Australian Open and the U.S. Open, giving him a total of four Grand Slam wins. The Federer Express, as some reporters had nicknamed him, was moving at full steam. With many of his goals accomplished, he sought to play the best tennis he could for as long as he could. On the way, he chased after the four tournament wins that would earn him a true Grand Slam series victory.

Over the next six years, his career would land him solidly in the record books. Reporters, fans, and other players would speak about him with awe. Many would say they thought he was the greatest tennis player of all time. Federer was at his peak, dominating the tennis world, and would not slow down for a long time.

## Chasing the Grand Slam

Beginning in 2004 many people believed that Federer might be able to accomplish a career Grand Slam—and maybe even a true Grand Slam. Rod Laver, the last man to win a true Grand Slam in 1969, reflected on the difficulty of winning the series of four tournaments in a single year. As he put it: "You have to be very

*Rafael Nadal of Spain consoles Federer during the trophy presentation after Federer's loss in the men's final match of the 2009 Australian Open.*

fortunate, avoid sickness, injuries. It's a nine-month task … [but Federer] has the potential to pull it off."[61]

In 2005, 2006, and 2007, Federer racked up a staggering number of Grand Slam wins (eight in a three-year period). In 2005, he won Wimbledon and the U.S. Open. In 2006 and 2007, he won the Australian Open, Wimbledon, and the U.S. Open in both years, giving him a total of twelve Grand Slam victories in his career. Despite these amazing results, a French Open victory continued to elude him. Without a win there, both a career Grand Slam and a true Grand Slam would remain only dreams.

The lack of a Grand Slam persisted in 2008. His year began poorly because of a case of mononucleosis. The Australian Open and the French Open slipped through his fingers. Even Wimbledon, which he had won five years in a row, passed him by when Rafael Nadal defeated him. His year finally turned around at the U.S. Open, where he won his thirteenth Grand Slam tournament.

At the beginning of 2009, Federer was twenty-seven years old—by some standards, past his prime as a tennis player. His chances for a Grand Slam were dwindling. Yet 2009 was not to be the year to make history; he was defeated in January in the final round of the Australian Open by Rafael Nadal, eliminating his chances of earning a true Grand Slam. Federer's best hope seemed to be to accomplish a career Grand Slam. To do that, he would need to win the French Open, which was just months away. Federer still had a shot.

## Conquering the French Open

The French Open was the only Grand Slam tournament Federer had never won. Rafael Nadal had defeated him there in 2006, 2007, and 2008. The unpredictable clay courts often gave Federer problems; he was much more comfortable on Wimbledon's grass courts.

In the 2009 tournament, Federer had help. Nadal was defeated by Robin Söderling in a match that shocked the tennis world and ended Nadal's French Open winning streak. Federer then faced Söderling, who was in excellent form, in the final round. The game was intense, as *Sports Illustrated* reporter S. L. Price noted: "Federer stood, then walked to the service line. A chorus of *shhhhhhs* coursed through the stadium. His thoughts were out of control now; almost in tears, he wished Söderling would spray four errors and make it easy." Federer served, and the championship point was in play. "The voices of 16,890 fell silent," wrote Price. "Federer bounced the ball, then cracked it down the T [court line]."[62] Söderling hit the ball into the net, giving Federer the win that had been beyond his reach for so long. He won the match and took the French Open title for the very first time.

Federer had finally achieved a career Grand Slam. He was just the sixth man in history to do so. In addition, thanks to the Olympic gold medal he had won in 2008, his career Grand Slam was also a career Golden Slam. If that was not enough, the win brought his Grand Slam total to fourteen, tying the record for Grand Slam titles held by Pete Sampras.

The finish was emotional for Federer. He accepted his trophy in the pouring rain on the clay courts of Paris and told reporters:

> Maybe my greatest victory—or certainly the one that takes the most pressure off my shoulders. I think that now, and until the end of my career, I can really play with my mind at peace and no longer hear that I've never won at Roland Garros [the French Open].[63]

## Continuing the Grand Slam Hunt

Once Federer tied Pete Sampras's record, onlookers wondered whether he could pull ahead to set a new record. His career was going strong and 2009 was only half over in the tennis circuit. He still had two chances to win another Grand Slam that year.

On the familiar grass courts at Wimbledon, Federer made his-

*Federer salutes spectators after victory in the men's singles final match against Andy Roddick in the 2009 Wimbledon Championships. This win was Federer's fifteenth Grand Slam title.*

# The History of Wimbledon

The annual grass-court tennis tournament known as Wimbledon is the oldest lawn tennis tournament in the world. It carries perhaps the most prestige of any current professional tournament. A win at Wimbledon is unofficially recognized as one of the greatest wins in tennis.

The first Lawn Tennis Championship was held in 1877 at the All England Club in London. Around 1900 the first international players participated. Since then the competition has expanded; it saw a surge in international popularity in the 1950s after air travel became more common. Some of the biggest names in tennis have enjoyed multiple Wimbledon wins, including Björn Borg, Pete Sampras (who shares the record for seven wins with W. C. Renshaw), and Roger Federer. Among women, Martina Navratilova holds the record with nine Wimbledon wins.

tory again. He captured his sixth Wimbledon title against Andy Roddick, giving him fifteen career Grand Slam wins and surpassing Pete Sampras's record. At the 2009 U.S. Open, he was defeated in the final round and was unable to further his new record. Still, 2009 was a memorable year that once again placed Federer in the record books. Following Wimbledon, a reporter asked him how it felt to win fifteen Grand Slam titles. In his typical modest fashion, he replied: "I like it. Makes me happy. I don't know. I mean, it's staggering, you know, that I've been able to play so well for, you know, so many years now."[64]

## Ruling the ATP Rankings

When Federer grabbed the number one ranking in 2004, the tennis world wondered how long he might hold on to that position. They would have a long wait: Federer ended up owning the top ranking for an astonishing 237 weeks in a row—more than four years. He bypassed the previous record of consecutive weeks, held by Jimmy Connors (with 160 consecutive weeks at number one) by a long shot. His reign as number one for most consecutive weeks ended on August 18, 2008, when he lost to Rafael Nadal at the Cincinnati Masters tournament, giving Nadal the top spot.

Having spent so much time as number one, another record waited to be broken. Pete Sampras owned the record for the most overall weeks at number one, having held the spot for a total of 286 weeks. If Federer could regain the number one ranking and

## The Greatest Match Ever Played

**R**oger Federer faced Rafael Nadal in the Wimbledon final in 2008, a match that would become known as the greatest match ever played. Reporters gushed over the intense perfection of play between the number one and number two ranked players in tennis. The match set a record for the longest final match in Wimbledon history, at four hours, forty-eight minutes. Nadal eventually took the title from defending champion Federer in five sets. Sportswriters sang the praises of both players, crediting their strength, perfection, and calm demeanor up until the last shot. Author L. Jon Wertheim did not hold back his admiration for both players and described them as executing one of the most perfect sporting events ever:

> . . . this match had it all. Skill . . . Courage . . . Self-sufficiency, sportsmanship, grace, discipline, gallantry, poise, intelligence, humility, injury, recovery, fibrillations of momentum, even acts of God. . . . The match was also significant for what it lacked: melodrama, trash talk, gamesmanship.

Quoted in L. Jon Wertheim. *Strokes of Genius—Federer, Nadal, and the Greatest Match Ever Played*. Boston: Houghton Mifflin Harcourt, 2009, p. 3.

keep it for at least fifty weeks, he could break Sampras's record.

From August 2008 until July 2009, Federer bounced between being number two and number three. When he returned to Wimbledon, his favorite Grand Slam tournament, and grabbed his sixth Wimbledon trophy, the victory moved him back into the number one ranking. Federer resumed his quest for the most overall weeks at number one, but he had a long way to go.

As the 2010 French Open got underway, Federer reached 285 total weeks at number one. The French Open would decide his fate. He reached the quarterfinal round, then struggled against his opponent Robin Söderling. Federer could not turn the match in his favor and lost the match.

Rafael Nadal, meanwhile, won against Söderling, making it Nadal's fifth French Open win. As the number 2 player in the world at that time, the win nudged him ahead of Federer, and he again took the number one spot on June 7, 2010. Federer was stopped short in his quest for the most weeks at number one, only one week away from a tie with Pete Sampras.

Throughout the rest of 2010 and into early 2011, Federer volleyed back and forth between number 2 and number 3, typically trading positions with Novak Djokovic of Serbia. But in May 2011 a climb back into the number one spot was not out of the question. Federer would need to play perfect tennis and win some major victories. Fans remained optimistic about another new record for Federer.

## Practically Perfect Style, Technique, and Artistry

Many tennis legends, heroes, and records have come and gone. Even with all Federer's victories and record-breaking accomplishments, one thing will always set him apart from other athletes. Tennis analysts, journalists, and competitors generally agree: Federer is the picture of perfect tennis.

His achievements, coupled with flawless moves, have led many observers to credit him with a perfect game. Time and again Federer is praised for having three assets: natural talent, an

*Federer's smooth techniques and flawless games make him the picture of perfect tennis.*

ability to adapt, and a true passion for training. Journalist Jeff Wortman is one person who has included Federer's love of the game as part of his successful recipe. As he put it: "There is a flourish to his groundstrokes and beauty to his movement. He just seems to enjoy the game. ... There is a sense that he might not even mind losing once in a while, as long as he enjoys himself."[65]

*Sports Illustrated* reporter L. Jon Wertheim points out one aspect of Federer's greatness. "Federer not only retrieves the most difficult shots," notes Wertheim, "but returns them with force and precision."[66] Former number three–ranked player Lleyton Hewitt agrees, saying, "He just doesn't give you any easy points."[67] Asked by an interviewer to analyze Federer's strokes, tennis great Boris Becker could find nothing to criticize. "I don't see a player in today's game who gets anywhere near the sort of volleys he is able to play." Becker also noted Federer's impressive speed and artful footwork: "He is so fast that out of a bad position he can make a good play and that's what I would call his biggest weapon. His speed and footwork means he almost comes across the court like a perfectly timed ballet dancer."[68]

Such skill, talent, and passion have earned Federer acknowledgement as the greatest tennis player of all time by the people who know him best: his colleagues and opponents. Among the tennis players who praise Federer are Andre Agassi, Björn Borg, Billie Jean King, John McEnroe, Robin Söderling, and even two-time Grand Slam winner Rod Laver. Reporters and analysts also honor Federer with this title, includ-

# Pete Sampras

**A**merican Pete Sampras played professionally for fifteen years, from 1988 to 2002, and was considered one of the greatest players of his time. He held the record for the most Grand Slam wins until 2009, when Roger Federer surpassed him with sixteen titles. Federer upset another of Sampras's records in 2001, when he knocked him out of the Wimbledon tournament, ending Sampras's 31-match winning streak at that competition. Sampras continues to hold the record for the most weeks as the number one ranked tennis player: Federer trails his record of 286 weeks by just a single week. Sampras retired from tennis in 2002.

Like many tennis players, Sampras supports charity. He is also an avid supporter of five other charities and has appeared in a number of celebrity tennis events for charity.

*Pete Sampras is all smiles following match point of the 2002 U.S. Open Final. Sampras won his 14th Grand Slam title, defeating Andre Agassi.*

ing Simon Barnes of London's *Sunday Times* and sports editors at CNN.com. Although some journalists, such as Wertheim, are reluctant to proclaim their opinion of the greatest tennis player ever, Federer's name dominates their articles and editorials. Many fans place Federer on a pedestal as well, as demonstrated at the 2007 Masters Cup in Shanghai, China, when Swiss fans held a banner that read: "Shhh! Quiet! Genius at work."[69]

## A Perfect Game, and a Personality to Match

Many tennis players have lost to Federer. They sometimes admit that they would love to hate him. Yet they typically admit that in spite of being beaten, they cannot help but like Federer, because he is such a nice guy. As American tennis player Andy Roddick once said, "I've told him before 'I'd love to hate you, but you're really nice.'"[70]

Reporters and analysts continually compliment Federer for his patience and thoughtful answers to interview questions. On-air commentators frequently remark on his calm demeanor and respect for line judges. While some players smash rackets or burst into tirades, as American John McEnroe was famous for doing, Federer remains steady and cool.

Some athletes appear polite in public but explode in private or tear apart opponents in interviews. Federer manages to avoid private fits. He is almost always complimentary of his opponents after a match, whether he wins or loses. He is considered a great role model not only in tennis, but in the world of sports and celebrities in general. UNICEF executive director Ann M. Veneman praised his reputation when she said, "Roger is not just a role model for aspiring athletes, but for all those who believe that we have the power and responsibility to make the world a better place."[71]

As a record-breaking tennis player, Federer would likely have a huge following of fans regardless of his personality. But many critics feel that his gentlemanly behavior makes him all the more appealing to fans. Sportswriter Simon Barnes put his thoughts

*Federer is credited with not only being a great tennis player, but also a great role model.*

about Federer's pleasant demeanor in the following way: "We love the brilliance of Roger Federer, but somehow his niceness makes it all the better."[72]

Throughout all of his success and record breaking, Federer has also managed to remain modest and appreciative of his good fortune. He reminds the tennis world of the hard work he endured to reach his peak, and he remembers his long climb to the top. He shows his appreciation for everyone who contributes on the tennis court, from the coaches to the judges and right down to the ball boys and girls. At his hometown tournament in Basel, where he was once a ball boy himself, he has established a tradition of throwing a pizza party for the ball boys and girls at the end of the contest. He spends time with the aspiring players, signs autographs, and lets them know that he appreciates their hard work. Federer's modesty is exemplified by a comment he made during a *60 Minutes* interview: "You can never be bigger than the game."[73]

## The Future of Federer

Athletes are continually asked how long they expect to keep playing and keep winning. Federer has often answered the question by looking ahead to 2012. His plan, he has told reporters, is to continue playing professionally and hope for a spot on the Swiss Olympic team. His sights are set on the Summer Games in London, where the tennis matches will be held on the grass courts at Wimbledon. With six wins at Wimbledon, he feels he has a good chance of reaching the medal rounds. Speculation has erupted that Federer, who will be thirty-one years old in 2012, will retire at the end of that year.

Federer does not see that as the end of his career. He told an interviewer, "I don't have a problem saying this is the second half of my career because I do have kids and a lot of things have changed around me," he said. "People think I'm going to retire at the 2012 Olympics—which is not true. . . . I would like to play beyond that so we'll see how it goes."[74] Meanwhile, the tennis world awaits the continuation of Federer's career and waits expectantly to see if he will expand his list of world records.

Roger Federer, blissful husband, proud father, and record-holding number one tennis player, would agree that he lives a charmed life. Yet somehow he keeps his feet on the ground while striving for huge goals. When asked by an interviewer for a piece of advice, Federer offered modestly, "Be true to yourself, honest and always try to do things for others less fortunate."[75] Federer lives and plays by these virtues, and this is what has made him great.

## Introduction: Becoming Roger Federer

1. Quoted in Liz Hayes. "Hot Stuff." *60 Minutes*, CBS, August 28, 2005. http://video.au.msn.com/watch/video/hot-stuff/xwczfey?cpkey=b1c755a4-4f43-4481-9e6f-227dbfcb7b16%7C%7C%7C.
2. Quoted in René Stauffer. *Roger Federer: Quest for Perfection.* New York: New Chapter, 2010, p. 20.
3. S.L. Price. "My Sportsman: Roger Federer." *Sports Illustrated,* November 27, 2009. http://sportsillustrated.cnn.com/2009/magazine/specials/sportsman/2009/11/25/price.sportsman/index.html.
4. Quoted in Credit Suisse. "Do It the Roger Federer Way." March 23, 2011. https://sponsorship.credit-suisse.com/app/article/index.cfm?fuseaction=OpenArticle&aoid=298942&video=true&void=298955&lang=EN.
5. Quoted in Billie Jean King. "Roger Federer." *Interview*, July 2006, p. 94.

## Chapter 1: Junior Tennis Phenomenon

6. Quoted in Stauffer. *Roger Federer,* p. 5.
7. Quoted in Stauffer. *Roger Federer,* p. 5.
8. Quoted in Stauffer. *Roger Federer,* p. 8.
9. Quoted in Thomas Stevens. "From Teenage Tantrums to Sublime Success." Swissinfo, November 29, 2010. www.swissinfo.ch/eng/Specials/Roger_Federer/Analysis/From_teenage_tantrums_to_sublime_success.html?cid=62098.
10. Quoted in Andreas Thomann. "Roger Federer on His Foundation." Credit Suisse, March 3, 2011. https://sponsorship.credit-suisse.com/app/article/index.cfm?fuseaction=OpenArticle&aoid=300952&coid-279860&lang-EN.
11. Stauffer. *Roger Federer,* p. 11.
12. Quoted in Stauffer. *Roger Federer,* p. 13.
13. Quoted in Roger Federer.com. "Ask Roger." www.rogerfederer.com/en/fanzone/askroger/qcat/4-juniorenzeit.html.
14. Quoted in Stauffer. *Roger Federer*, p. 23.

15.    Quoted in Stephen Tignor. "Federer Express." *Tennis,* Vol. 35, Iss. 5, 1999.

## Chapter 2: Federer Steps Up to the Pros

16.    Quoted in Mark Lamport-Stokes. "New Wave of Young Guns Excites Roger Federer at Indian Wells." Reuters, March 16, 2011. www.reuters.com/article/2011/03/16/us-tennis-indian-men-federer-idUSTRE72F1AK20110316.
17.    Quoted in King. "Roger Federer," p. 66.
18.    Quoted in Hayes. "Hot Stuff."
19.    Quoted in ASAP Sports. "Wimbledon: Roger Federer." July 2, 2001. www.asapsports.com/show_interview.php?id=21605.
20.    Quoted in Cindy Shmerler. "The Artful Roger." *Tennis,* Vol. 39, Iss. 2, 2003, p. 28.
21.    Quoted in Tim Adams. "It'll All End in Tears…." *Observer* (UK), August 1, 2004. http://observer.guardian.co.uk/osm/story/0,,1270865,00.html.
22.    Quoted in Steven Howard. "Roger Federer." *Sun* (UK), July 7, 2003, p. 52.
23.    Quoted in Shmerler. "The Artful Roger." *Tennis,* Vol. 39, Iss. 2, 2003, p. 28.
24.    Quoted in Sporting Life.com. "Federer Is the Future—Becker." www.sportinglife.com/tennis/wimbledon2003/news/story_get.cgi?STORY_NAME=wimbledon/03/07/06/WIMBLEDON_Federer_Reaction.html.
25.    Quoted in Associated Press. "Swiss Success." *SI.com,* July 7, 2003. http://sportsillustrated.cnn.com/tennis/2003/wimbledon/news/2003/07/06/wimbledon_sunday_ap.
26.    Quoted in ASAP Sports. "Australian Open: Roger Federer." February 1, 2004. www.asapsports.com/show_interview.php?id=21463.
27.    Quoted in Stauffer. *Roger Federer,* p. 107.
28.    Quoted in Allen St. John. "MISSION: Possible." *Tennis,* October 2004, p. 52.
29.    Quoted in St. John. "MISSION: Possible," p. 52.

## Chapter 3: The Pursuit of Gold

30.    Quoted in Stauffer. *Roger Federer,* p. 42.

31. Quoted in ASAP Sports. "Olympic Tennis Tournament: Roger Federer." August 17, 2004. www.asapsports.com/ show_interview.php?id=21415.

32. Quoted in Kaz Mochlinski. "Roger Federer Seeks Greatness at Beijing Olympics." *Telegraph* (UK), August 9, 2009. http://blogs.telegraph.co.uk/sport/kazmochlinski/4845137/ Roger_Federer_seeks_greatness_at_Beijing_Olympics.

33. Quoted in Official Website of the Beijing 2008 Olympic Games. "Roger Federer: Olympic Love Game." August 10, 2008. http://en.beijing2008.cn/news/special/features/ n214525565.shtml.

34. Quoted in Olympic.org. "The Best of Us." Video. www .olympic.org/the-best-of-us?tab=1.

35. David Cox. "Imperial Federer Re-establishes Order." Tennistalk.com, August 12, 2008. www.tennistalk.com/en/ match_report/Olympic_Games/2008/Roger_Federer_-_ Dmitry_Tursunov.

36. Quoted in Roger Federer.com. "Roger Wins Olympic Gold Medal." August 16, 2008. www.rogerfederer.com/en/esp/ news-detail/news/728-roger-gewinnt-gold-im-doppel .html?tx_comments_pi1[page]=4&cHash=0240eb562bc2 7aad823db3cb1a1352ee.

## Chapter 4: Behind the Scenes

37. Quoted in King. "Roger Federer," p. 94.

38. Quoted in Ivan Turmo. "Working with Federer Was Not Always Easy." Swissinfo, August 30, 2009. www.swissinfo. ch/eng/Specials/Roger_Federer/Analysis/Working_with_ Federer_was_not_always_easy.html?cid=62100.

39. Quoted in Bill Scott. "Working Out with Roger Federer." Tennis.com, December 9, 2008. www.tennis.com/articles/ templates/fitness.aspx?articleid=1149&zoneid=19.

40. Quoted in ASAP Sports. "Wimbledon: Roger Federer." June 25, 2006. www.asapsports.com/show_interview .php?id=36016.

41. Quoted in Felix Latzer, "Auch im Wort-Tennis Weltklasse." *Schweitzer Illustrierte Online*, October 31, 2009. Translated by Anne K. Brown. www.schweizer-illustrierte.ch/people/ auch-im-wort-tennis-weltklasse.

42. Quoted in Roger Federer.com. "Ask Roger."

43. Quoted in ASAP Sports. "U.S. Open: Roger Federer." September 1, 2007. www.asapsports.com/show_interview .php?id=45286.

44. Quoted in C. Christopher. "TENNIS: Federer Stays in Control, On and Off the Court." *New York Times,* May 21, 2005, p. 1.

45. Quoted in Roger Federer.com. "Ask Roger." http://www .rogerfederer.com/en/fanzone/askroger.html.

46. Quoted in Hayes. "Hot Stuff."

47. Quoted in Richard Jago. "Roger Federer Has New Twin Priorities." *Guardian* (UK), August 20, 2009. www.guardian .co.uk/sport/2009/aug/20/roger-federer-cincinnati-masters.

48. Lindt. "A Perfect Match: Roger Federer to Become Global Ambassador for His Favorite Chocolate: Lindt." October 29, 2009. www.lindtusa.com/info-exec/display/ pressrogerfederer.

49. Quoted in Credit Suisse. "Roger Federer Poses for Star Photographer Testino." March 1, 2011. https://multimedia .credit-suisse.com/index.cfm?fuseaction=OpenMultimedia &aoid=299590&coid=258927&media=video&lang=EN.

## Chapter 5: Tennis Star and Humanitarian

50. Quoted in King. "Roger Federer," p. 94.

51. Quoted in King. "Roger Federer," p. 94.

52. Quoted in Thomas Stevens. "Solid Foundation Improves Children's Lives." Swissinfo. June 11, 2009. www.swissinfo .ch/eng/Specials/Roger_Federer/Analysis/Solid_foundation_ improves_childrens_lives.html?cid=62106.

53. Quoted in Stevens. "Solid Foundation Improves Children's Lives."

54. Quoted in Roger Federer Foundation. "Mission: 'I Am Tomorrow's Future.'" www.rogerfedererfoundation.org/en/ foundation/mission.

55. Quoted in Roger Federer Shop. "Roger Federer Foundation." www.rogerfederershop.com/en/foundation.html.

56. Jon Wertheim. "Top 10 Tennis Stories of 2010." *SI.com,* December 26, 2010. http://sportsillustrated.cnn.com/2010/ writers/jon_wertheim/12/21/top10.stories/index. html#ixzz1GgTbejlt.

57. Quoted in Deepti Patwardhan. "We Won't See a Player

like Federer in the Next 100 Years." Rediff.com, January 4, 2006. www.rediff.com/sports/2006/jan/04allegro.htm.

58. Quoted in Sabine Dolan. "UNICEF's Newest Goodwill Ambassador, Tennis Star Roger Federer, Hits an Ace for Children." UNICEF, April 3, 2006. www.unicef.org/infobycountry/usa_32007.html.

59. Quoted in Dolan. "UNICEF's Newest Goodwill Ambassador, Tennis Star Roger Federer, Hits an Ace for Children."

60. Quoted in Roger Federer Foundation. "Governance." www.rogerfedererfoundation.org/en/foundation/organization.

## Chapter 6: Still Swinging

61. Quoted in St. John. "MISSION: Possible."

62. S.L. Price. "Is He the Greatest of All Time?" *Sports Illustrated,* June 15, 2009. http://sportsillustrated.cnn.com/vault/article/magazine/MAG1156168/index.htm.

63. Quoted in Howard Fendrich. "2009 French Open Winner: Roger Federer Beats Soderling to Tie Sampras' Record." *Huffington Post,* June 7, 2009. www.huffingtonpost.com/2009/06/07/2009-french-open-winner-r_n_212313.html.

64. Quoted in ASAP Sports. "Wimbledon: Roger Federer." July 5, 2009. www.asapsports.com/show_interview.php?id=57650.

65. Jeff Wortman. "Passionless Pete Pales Next to Roger's Joie de Vivre." *Age* (Melbourne), November 22, 2007, p. 12.

66. L. Jon Wertheim. "Racket Boss." *Sports Illustrated*, October 4, 2004, p. 78.

67. Quoted in Wertheim. "Racket Boss," p. 78.

68. Quoted in BBC Sports. "Does Federer Have the Perfect Game?" July 6, 2009. http://news.bbc.co.uk/sport2/hi/tennis/8135134.stm.

69. Quoted in Associated Press. "Federer Wins 4th Masters Cup Crown in 5 Years." NBC Sports, November 18, 2007. http://nbcsports.msnbc.com/id/21844884.

70. Quoted in *USA Today.* "Roddick: Federer Might Be Greatest Player Ever." July 5, 2005. www.usatoday.com/sports/tennis/wimb/2005-07-03-roddick-marvels_x.htm.

71.     Quoted in UNICEF. "UNICEF Appoints Tennis Champion Roger Federer as Goodwill Ambassador." April 3, 2006. www.unicef.org/media/media_32001.html.
72.     Simon Barnes. "Roger Federer Proves Nice Guys Can Finish First at Wimbledon." *Sunday Times* (London), June 26, 2009. www.timesonline.co.uk/tol/sport/columnists/simon_barnes/article6578508.ece.
73.     Quoted in Hayes. "Hot Stuff."
74.     Quoted in Jonathan Overend. "Roger Federer vows to keep playing beyond Olympics." British Broadcasting Company, May 13, 2010, http://news.bbc.co.uk/sport2/hi/8678609.stm.
75.     Quoted in Chris Beastall. "Ape to Gentleman Interview Roger Federer." Ape to Gentleman, October 27, 2010. www.apetogentleman.com/apeish/ape-to-gentleman-interview-roger-federer.

**1981**

Roger Federer is born in Basel, Switzerland, on August 8.

**1984**

At age three, gets his first taste of tennis; within a few months he is able to hit a ball over the net.

**1987**

Joins a local tennis club and is recognized as the best player in his age group; receives extra lessons and soon begins tournament play; is an avid watcher of tennis matches on television.

**1993**

Wins his first Swiss national junior title and a second national title six months later; decides to abandon the sport of soccer.

**1995**

The Swiss National Tennis Center at Ecublens accepts Roger as a student, and he moves across the country.

**1996**

At age fifteen he wins the Swiss national junior title in the sixteen-and-under division.

**1997**

Wins both the indoor and outdoor 1997 Swiss national junior championships in the eighteen-and-under division; moves to the new Swiss National Tennis Center in Biel; appears on the ATP rankings for the first time at number 803.

**1998**

Wins the Wimbledon junior championships; finishes the year as the number one ranked junior player in the world and is ranked number 301 by the ATP.

**1999**

Turns professional with an ATP ranking of 301 and achieves startling results at an open tournament in Marseille, France; beats reigning French Open winner Carlos Moyá in his first round; his ATP ranking rises to 129, and he finishes the year ranked number sixty-five.

## 2000

A trip to the Olympic Games in Sydney, Australia, is a disappointment; makes the medal rounds but finishes in fourth place; his ATP ranking continues to rise, and he finishes the year ranked number twenty-nine; meets Mirka Vavrinec, and the two begin dating.

## 2001

Continues on the professional circuit; plays well but wins only one ATP title at the Milan Indoors tournament; finishes the year ranked number thirteen; the highlight of his year is defeating Pete Sampras at Wimbledon.

## 2002

Is devastated by the news that his friend and former coach Peter Carter was killed in a car crash while on vacation in South Africa; receives an invitation to the prestigious Tennis Masters Cup and ends the year ranked number six.

## 2003

Accomplishes his dream of winning at Wimbledon, his first Grand Slam title; becomes the fourth player in history to win both junior and gentleman's singles titles at Wimbledon; finishes the year ranked number two by the ATP; establishes the Roger Federer Foundation.

## 2004

Wins three more Grand Slam titles, at the Australian Open, Wimbledon, and the U.S. Open; participates in the Olympic Games in Athens but returns home without a medal; is ranked the number one player by the ATP for the entire year.

## 2005

Again spends the year ranked number one; wins two Grand Slam tournaments, at Wimbledon and the U.S. Open.

## 2006

Takes home three Grand Slam trophies, from the Australian

Open, Wimbledon, and the U.S. Open; his ranking remains at number one throughout the year.

## 2007

Becomes the first living person featured on a Swiss postage stamp; his year is a duplicate of 2006, as he remains at number one and wins the Australian Open, Wimbledon, and the U.S. Open.

## 2008

Has a bumpy year that starts with illness from mononucleosis; his epic match against Rafael Nadal at Wimbledon is featured on the cover of *Sports Illustrated;* keeps hold of his number one ranking until August, when he moves to number two; attends the Olympic Games and goes home with a gold medal in men's doubles; his only Grand Slam tournament win is at the U.S. Open.

## 2009

For the first time, wins the French Open, giving him a Career Grand Slam; is featured on the cover of *Sports Illustrated* with the caption "Master Stroke, Winning the French, Roger Federer Makes His Case as the Best Ever"; in July he moves back into the number one ranking; wins at Wimbledon, giving him fifteen career Grand Slam wins and the world record for the most Grand Slam wins; marries his girlfriend, Mirka; their twin daughters are born in July.

## 2010

Wins his sixteenth Grand Slam tournament, at the Australian Open; remains in the number one ranking until June, when he drops to number two; the Austrian postal service honors him by placing his image on a postage stamp; plays his nine hundredth professional tennis match.

## 2011

His ranking shifts between number two and number three; he begins to make plans for the Olympic Summer Games in London in 2012.

# For More Information

## Books

Chris Bowers. *Roger Federer: Spirit of a Champion.* London: John Blake, 2009. A thorough biography of Roger Federer from his youth and early tennis years up to 2008.

Chris Bowers. *Roger Federer: The Greatest.* London: John Blake, 2010. A revised and updated version of *Roger Federer: Spirit of a Champion* that details his career into 2010.

René Stauffer. *Roger Federer: Quest for Perfection.* New York: New Chapter, 2010. A complete biography of Federer by Swiss journalist René Stauffer that traces his life and career from childhood through 2010.

L. Jon Wertheim. *Strokes of Genius—Federer, Nadal, and the Greatest Match Ever Played.* Boston: Houghton Mifflin Harcourt, 2009. A detailed account of every facet of the epic match between Roger Federer and Rafael Nadal at Wimbledon in 2008.

## Periodicals

C. Christopher. "TENNIS: Federer Stays in Control, On and Off the Court." *New York Times,* May 21, 2005.

Billie Jean King. "Roger Federer." *Interview,* July 2006.

S.L. Price. "He Stands Alone." *Sports Illustrated,* January 17, 2005.

S.L. Price. "My Sportsman: Roger Federer." *Sports Illustrated,* November 27, 2009.

Cindy Shmerler. "The Artful Roger." *Tennis,* Vol. 39, Iss. 2, 2003.

Stephen Tignor. "Federer Express." *Tennis,* Vol. 35, Iss. 5, 1999.

L. Jon Wertheim. "Racket Boss." *Sports Illustrated,* October 4, 2004.

Jeff Wortman. "Passionless Pete Pales Next to Roger's Joie de Vivre." *Age* (Melbourne), November 22, 2007.

## Internet Sources

Tim Adams. "It'll All End in Tears...." *Observer* (UK), August 1, 2004. http://observer.guardian.co.uk/osm/story/0,,1270865,00.html.

Associated Press. "Federer Wins 4th Masters Cup Crown in 5 Years." NBC Sports, November 18, 2007. http://nbcsports.msnbc.com/id/21844884.

Simon Barnes. "Roger Federer Proves Nice Guys Can Finish First at Wimbledon." *Sunday Times* (London), June 26, 2009. www.timesonline.co.uk/tol/sport/columnists/simon_barnes/article6578508.ece.

BBC Sports. "Does Federer Have the Perfect Game?" July 6, 2009. http://news.bbc.co.uk/sport2/hi/tennis/8135134.stm.

Chris Beastall. "Ape to Gentleman Interview Roger Federer." Ape to Gentlemen, October 27, 2010. www.apetogentleman.com/apeish/ape-to-gentleman-interview-roger-federer.

David Cox. "Imperial Federer Re-establishes Order." Tennistalk.com, August 12, 2008. www.tennistalk.com/en/match_report/Olympic_Games/2008/Roger_Federer_-_Dmitry_Tursunov.

Credit Suisse. "Roger Federer Poses for Star Photographer Testino." March 1, 2011. https://multimedia.credit-suisse.com/index.cfm?fuseaction=OpenMultimedia&aoid=299590&coid=258927&media=video&lang=EN.

Credit Suisse. "Do It the Roger Federer Way." March 23, 2011. https://sponsorship.credit-suisse.com/app/article/index.cfm?fuseaction=OpenArticle&aoid=298942&video=true&void=298955&lang=EN.

Sabine Dolan. "UNICEF's Newest Goodwill Ambassador, Tennis Star Roger Federer, Hits an Ace for Children." UNICEF, April 3, 2006. www.unicef.org/infobycountry/usa_32007.html.

Howard Fendrich. "2009 French Open Winner: Roger Federer Beats Soderling to Tie Sampras' Record." *Huffington Post,* June 7, 2009. www.huffingtonpost.com/2009/06/07/2009-french-open-winner-r_n_212313.html.

Richard Jago. "Roger Federer Has New Twin Priorities." *Guardian* (UK), August 20, 2009. www.guardian.co.uk/sport/2009/aug/20/roger-federer-cincinnati-masters.

Mark Lamport-Stokes. "New Wave of Young Guns Excites Roger Federer at Indian Wells." Reuters, March 16, 2011. www .reuters.com/article/2011/03/16/us-tennis-indian-men-federer-idUSTRE72F1AK20110316.

Lindt. "A Perfect Match: Roger Federer to Become Global Ambassador for His Favorite Chocolate: Lindt." October 29, 2009. www.lindtusa.com/info-exec/display/pressrogerfederer.

Kaz Mochlinski. "Roger Federer Seeks Greatness at Beijing Olympics." *Telegraph* (UK), August 9, 2009. http://blogs .telegraph.co.uk/sport/kazmochlinski/4845137/Roger_ Federer_seeks_greatness_at_Beijing_Olympics.

Jonathan Overend. "Roger Federer Vows to Keep Playing Beyond Olympics." BBC Sport, May 13, 2010. http://news.bbc.co.uk/ sport2/hi/8678609.stm.

Deepti Patwardhan. "We Won't See a Player like Federer in the Next 100 Years." Rediff.com, January 4, 2006. www.rediff.com/ sports/2006/jan/04allegro.htm.

Bill Scott. "Working Out with Roger Federer." Tennis.com, December 9, 2008. www.tennis.com/articles/templates/fitness. aspx?articleid=1149&zoneid=19.

Sporting Life.com. "Federer Is the Future—Becker." www .sportinglife.com/tennis/wimbledon2003/news/story_get .cgi?STORY_NAME=wimbledon/03/07/06/WIMBLEDON_ Federer_Reaction.html.

Thomas Stevens. "Solid Foundation Improves Children's Lives." Swissinfo. June 11, 2009. www.swissinfo.ch/eng/Specials/ Roger_Federer/Analysis/Solid_foundation_improves_childrens _lives.html?cid=62106.

Thomas Stevens. "From Teenage Tantrums to Sublime Success." Swissinfo, November 29, 2010. www.swissinfo.ch/eng/ Specials/Roger_Federer/Analysis/From_teenage_tantrums_to_ sublime_success.html?cid=62098.

Andreas Thomann. "Roger Federer on His Foundation." Credit Suisse. https://sponsorship.credit-suisse.com/app/article/ index.cfm?fuseaction=OpenArticle&aoid=300952&coid=27 9860&lang=EN.

Ivan Turmo. "Working with Federer Was Not Always Easy." Swissinfo, August 30, 2009. www.swissinfo.ch/eng/Specials/

Roger_Federer/Analysis/Working_with_Federer_was_not_
always_easy.html?cid=62100.

*USA Today.* "Roddick: Federer Might Be Greatest Player Ever."
July 5, 2005. www.usatoday.com/sports/tennis/wimb/2005-07-
03-roddick-marvels_x.htm.

Jon Wertheim. "Top 10 Tennis Stories of 2010." *SI.com,* December
26, 2010. http://sportsillustrated.cnn.com/2010/writers/jon_
wertheim/12/21/top10.stories/index.html#ixzz1GgTbejlt.

## Websites

**ASAP Sports** (www.asapsports.com). A website that is contract-
ed by major sports organizations, such as the ATP, NBA, and
NFL, to record and transcribe player press conferences following major sporting events.

**ATP World Tour** (www.atpworldtour.com). The official website
of the ATP, with complete statistics and ranking history of all
ATP players.

**Go Roger! The Roger Federer Fan site** (www.goroger.net). A
website that tracks the career of Roger Federer and includes
photos, interviews, articles, and videos.

**Jura** (www.ch.jura.com/home_ch_x.htm). The website of Jura,
one of Federer's sponsors. The website is in German; click on
"Unternehmen & Presse" to watch videos of Federer's activities
recorded by this manufacturer of coffeemakers.

**Roger Federer.com** (www.rogerfederer.com). The official website of Roger Federer, this site posts news, tournament results,
videos, and a year-by-year summary of Federer's career since
1995, as well as links to merchandise and the Roger Federer
Foundation.

**Roger Federer Foundation** (www.rogerfedererfoundation.org).
The official website of Roger Federer's charitable organization.
It provides instructions for donations and tracks the progress
of the foundation's efforts.

**Roger Federer Points** (www.rogerfedererpoints.com/profile. htm). Subtitled "Home of the Roger Federer Points Videos," this website offers news, background, photos, and videos of Roger Federer.

**Roger Federer the Champ** (http://rogerfedererthechamp. blogspot.com). A fan website devoted to Roger Federer, with recent news, photos, videos, history, schedules, and links.

# Picture Credits

Cover Photo, Vincent Kessler/Reuters/Landov
ADRIAN DENNIS/AFP/Getty Images, 10
AP Images/Amy Sancetta, 31
AP Images/Martin Gnedt, 36
Bob Thomas/Getty Images, 22
Catherine Servel/The Image Bank/Getty Images, 29
© Christian Liewig/Liewig Media Sports/Corbis, 84-85
Clive Brunskill/Getty Images, 57
© CORBIS, 16
© CSPA/NewSport/Corbis, 88
© Derek Croucher / Alamy, 14
© Duomo/CORBIS, 86
© EXPA/ David Rawcliffe/NewSport/Corbis, 62
© Francisco Martinez / Alamy, 13
GERRY PENNY/AFP/Getty Images, 34
Getty Images for ATP, 75
© imagebroker / Alamy, 55
© Jacques Langevin/Sygma/Corbis, 28
Jamie McDonald/Getty Images, 24
Jeff J Mitchell/Reuters /Landov, 39
Julian Finney/Getty Images, 52
Kevork Djansezian/Getty Images, 71
Matthew Stockman/Getty Images, 66
Paul Gilham/Getty Images, 80
© PCN Photography / Alamy, 20
© Robert Harding Picture Library Ltd / Alamy, 44
Robert Laberge/Getty Images, 46
Roger Federer Foundation via Getty images, 69
Scott Barbour/Getty Images, 78
SHAUN BEST/Reuters /Landov, 49
© Stephane Cardinale/People Avenue/Corbis, 72
© TAO Images Limited / Alamy, 43
© Victor Fraile/Corbis, 60

Anne K. Brown has kept busy as an editor and author for more than twenty years. She has worked on a wide range of publications ranging from trading cards to full-length novels. A highlight of her career was working for a major publisher of fantasy role-playing games, where she interacted with a number of quirky creative geniuses on a daily basis.

Brown holds a bachelor of arts degree in communication from the University of Wisconsin–Milwaukee. She spends her time with her husband, two daughters, and a spoiled black cat. She volunteers as a Girl Scout leader and a forensics coach.